National 5
Computing
Science

How to Pass

NATIONAL 5
Computing Science

Frank Frame

HODDER
GIBSON
AN HACHETTE UK COMPANY

The Publishers would like to thank the following for permission to reproduce copyright material:

Photo credits: p.91 © Mozilla; p.94–96 (all) Copyright © 2011 Microsoft Corporation and/or its suppliers, One Microsoft Way, Redmond, Washington 98052-6399 U.S.A. All rights reserved.; p.102 © 2010 Future Publishing / Getty Images; p.112 Copyright © 2013 members of the Audacity development team. Licensed under the Creative Commons Attribution License, version 3.0. "Audacity" is a trademark of Dominic Mazzoni.; p.114 Adobe product screenshot(s) reprinted with permission from Adobe Systems Incorporated.; p.115 (top) © Sergey Dashkevich – Fotolia, (bottom) © ktsdesign – Fotolia; p.117 (top) © iStockphoto.com/ Tatiana Popova, (bottom) © Dinostock – Fotolia; p.118 (top to bottom) DVD logo is a trademark of DVD Format/Logo Licensing Corporation, which is registered in the U.S., Japan and other countires., © Artur Synenko – Fotolia.com, © anubis3211 – Fotolia.com, © Siede Preis/Photodisc/ Getty Images / Tools of the Trade OS48, © Dmitry Terentjev – Fotolia; p.119 (top to bottom) © iStockphoto.com/216Photo, © Aaron Amat – Fotolia.com, © Entropia – Fotolia, © JackF – Fotolia, © Sascha Burkard – Fotolia.com; p.120 (top to bottom) © Mariusz Blach – Fotolia, © iStockphoto.com/ sweetym, © iStockphoto.com/Greg Nicholas; p.121 (top) © Dragan Radojkovic – Fotolia.com, (bottom) © Maxim_Kazmin – Fotolia; p.122 (top to bottom) © Fatman73 – Fotolia, © bloomua – Fotolia, © pizuttipics – Fotolia; p.124 (left) Ubuntu® is a trademark of Canonical Ltd and is used under licence from Canonical Ltd. Points of view or opinions in this publications do not necessarily represent the views, opinions, policies or positions of Canonical Ltd or imply any affiliation with Ubuntu or the Ubuntu project; p.125 (top) © Scanrail – Fotolia, (bottom) © Datacraft Co Ltd / Getty Images; p.131 (right) Copyright @ ESTsoft Corp. All Rights Reserved, (bottom) © Dino Ablakovic/istockphoto; p.133 © Crown Copyright; p.136 © Blend Images / Alamy; p.137 (top) Copyright © 2013, Intel Corporation. All rights reserved. Used with permission., (bottom) © lunamarina – Fotolia.com.

All screenshots taken using Scratch, in chapters 1, 3 and the Answers, are reproduced under a Creative Commons Attribution Share-Alike 3.0 licence (http://creativecommons.org/licenses/by-sa/3.0/legalcode). Scratch is a project of the Lifelong Kindergarten Group at the MIT Media Lab.

All screenshots and boxshots taken of Microsoft® software and packaging are used with permission from Microsoft.

All screenshots taken of Mozilla® software are copyright of the Mozilla Foundation.

The two tables of 'Mandatory Course Content for National 5 Computing Science' on pages 142–143 are quoted from the 'National 5 Computing Science Course Assessment Specification' document and are reproduced by permission of SQA. This document is available to view online at http://www.sqa.org.uk/files_ccc/CfE_CourseAssessSpec_N5_Technologies_ComputingScience.pdf.

Every effort has been made to trace all copyright holders, but if any have been inadvertently overlooked the Publishers will be pleased to make the necessary arrangements at the first opportunity.

Although every effort has been made to ensure that website addresses are correct at time of going to press, Hodder Gibson cannot be held responsible for the content of any website mentioned in this book. It is sometimes possible to find a relocated web page by typing in the address of the home page for a website in the URL window of your browser.

Hachette UK's policy is to use papers that are natural, renewable and recyclable products and made from wood grown in sustainable forests. The logging and manufacturing processes are expected to conform to the environmental regulations of the country of origin.

Orders: please contact Bookpoint Ltd, 130 Park Drive, Abingdon, Oxon OX14 4SE. Telephone: (44) 01235 827720.
Fax: (44) 01235 400454. Lines are open 9.00–5.00, Monday to Saturday, with a 24-hour message answering service. Visit our website at www.hoddereducation.co.uk. Hodder Gibson can be contacted direct on: Tel: 0141 848 1609; Fax: 0141 889 6315; email: hoddergibson@hodder.co.uk

© Frank Frame 2013

First published in 2013 by
Hodder Gibson, an imprint of Hodder Education,
An Hachette UK Company
2a Christie Street
Paisley PA1 1NB

Impression number		5	4	3	2	1
Year		2017	2016	2015	2014	2013

Cover photo © vege – Fotolia.com
Illustrations by Aptara, Inc.
Typeset in Cronos Pro by Aptara, Inc.
Printed in Spain
A catalogue record for this title is available from the British Library
ISBN: 978 1 444 18203 3

Contents

Introduction

This book is designed to help you pass Computing Science National 4 and National 5.

It covers all the mandatory content in the Software Design and Development unit at National 5 (see Appendix) including programming guides and examples, all that you need to know about reading and interpreting code as well as researching and reporting at National 4, and comparing software development environments at National 5.

It also covers all the mandatory content in the Information System Design and Development unit at National 5 (see Appendix) including Creating an Information System, Macros, Scripting and Mark-up Languages, Text, Graphics, Sound, and Video, Hardware, Networks and Security as well as The Law and the Environment.

It then focuses on:
- the added value unit for National 4
- the added value coursework and external exam for National 5, and provides guidance and exam preparation tips.

Note to teacher: Chapter 1 (Developing Software using Scratch) and Chapter 2 (Developing Software using Visual Basic) were written to suit Scratch version 1.4 and Visual Studio 5 respectively.

How this course is assessed

At National 4, all aspects of the Computing Science course are internally assessed.

At National 5, the Computing Science course is examined through two components: a question paper and an assignment.

The question paper

The National 5 question paper is set and marked by SQA, and will be given under exam conditions. The paper contains questions worth a total of 90 marks and is worth 60% of your overall grade. The paper is divided into two sections, which you will have a total of 1 hour and 30 minutes to complete.

Section 1:
- contains 20 marks
- consists of short answer questions to assess your knowledge.

Section 2:
- contains 70 marks
- consists of extended response questions to assess your understanding.

Across both sections, approximately half of the marks will relate to questions on Software Design and Development (Unit 1 in this book), and the other half will relate to questions on Information System Design and Development (Unit 2 in this book).

The paper is designed to test your knowledge of the course content and how you apply your knowledge and skills to context-based and problem-solving questions. A table of mandatory course content (reproduced courtesy of SQA) is provided in the appendix to this book, which gives details of all the topics you must cover as you go through the course.

The assignment

The National 5 assignment is titled 'Developing a Computing Science Solution' and is set by SQA under open-book conditions, marked internally by your teacher. In it your task is to analyse a computing science problem, design a solution to this problem, then implement, test and report on your solution.

There are 60 marks available in the assignment and it is worth 40% of your overall grade. Your teacher will be able to give you guidance and support through the planning stages of your assignment, and will instruct you on how to compile and submit your completed piece of work. Make sure you work at your best when undertaking the assignment – it can give you a solid platform from which to tackle the exam.

Hints & tips ★

Here are some handy tips for exam preparation:

✓ Draw up a revision plan well ahead of the exam. Make sure you create a schedule that lets you cover all of the topics, without leaving everything to the last minute.

✓ Use a checklist to make sure you cover all of the course content.

✓ Make sure you know all the important definitions in this book. (The Index will help you to find them!)

✓ Check that your knowledge is up to exam standards by answering all of the questions in this book. (Suggested answers are at the back!)

For National 5 Students

Many sections of this book are highlighted as being appropriate for National 4 study, but please note that these National 4 sections will often, indeed usually, form an important basis for National 5 study as well, and should not be overlooked!

Important!

The book you are holding is from the 2nd (or a subsequent) printing of this title. Certain pages have been changed from the first printing because of syllabus amendments that were made after the book was first published. Pages 142 to 143 now contain updated versions of the Mandatory Course Content for National 5, and related amendments in the text can be found on pages 83 and 135.

As detailed on the inner front cover of this book, always check www.sqa.org.uk for the most up to date course specifications.

Unit 1 Software Design and Development

Chapter 1
Developing Software using Scratch

Getting numbers into your program

In this section you are going to learn how to get whole numbers into your program.

Making a variable to store whole numbers

Using the *variables* window you can make and name a variable as shown in the screenshot below. You can even set, change, show and hide variables.

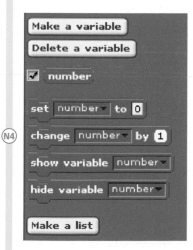

N4

Make a variable and call it *Number* as shown in the screenshot above. Open the *sensing* window and use the *ask and answer* blocks to enter a number.

1

The number you enter will appear on the screen as shown in the screenshot below:

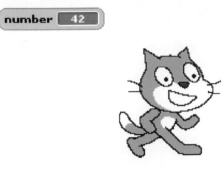

Save your program as Example1.

Activities

1 Write a program that asks for and displays the number of people in your family. Save it as Scratch Activity 1.
2 Write a program that asks for and displays the number of hours you watch television each day. Save it as Scratch Activity 2.
3 Create a program that:
   - enters the cost of a mobile phone
   - enters the cost of a games app for a phone.

(N4)

Assigning variables

This means you can set the value of a number. In Scratch you do this by using the *set* block.

This block assigns a number to the variable *cost of 1 phone call* as shown in the screenshot below.

```
set  cost of 1 phone call ▾  to  10
```

This block assigns a number to the variable *cost of 1 text message* as shown in the screenshot below:

```
set  cost of 1 text message ▾  to  4
```

Enter the program from the screenshot below:

```
when     clicked
set  cost of 1 phone call ▾  to  10
set  cost of 1 text message ▾  to  4
say  the cost of a phone call in pence is  for  1  secs
say  cost of 1 phone call  for  1  secs
say  the cost of a text message in pence is  for  1  secs
say  cost of 1 text message  for  1  secs
```

4 Write a program to assign and display:
  • the number of pupils in your class today
  • the number of boys in your class
  • the number of girls in your class.
Save it as Scratch Activity 4.

Output showing numeric variables

There are four ways to display a variable using Scratch.

The first three are available on the *popup* menu linked to each variable as shown in the screenshot below.

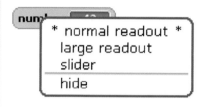

• Normal
• Large
• Slider

(N4) The fourth is produced by using a block from the *looks* window which causes the sprite to output the variable as shown in the screenshots below.

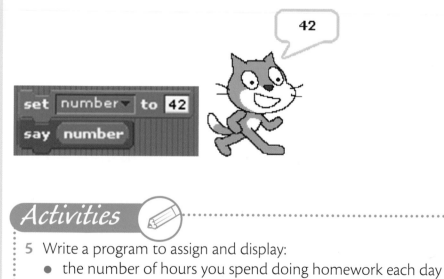

Activities

5 Write a program to assign and display:
  • the number of hours you spend doing homework each day
  • the number of hours you spend on the Internet each day
  • the number of hours you spend sleeping each night.
You must display each one in a different way. Save it as Scratch Activity 5.

Getting words into your program

Variables can hold words. They are called string variables. In Scratch you make a string variable in exactly the same way as you make a variable to hold a number. Make a variable called *Name*.

Enter the program from the screenshot below:

Your screen should look something like the screenshot below when you run it:

You can also use the sprite to display your string. Add this block your program:

Activities

6 Write a program that asks for and displays the title of a song. Save it as Scratch Activity 6.

7 Write a program that asks for and displays the name of a book. Save it as Scratch Activity 7.

Getting words and numbers into your program

This is easy in Scratch! You simply make the variables you want and then set them to the name or number or use the *ask/answer* to enter them.

Enter the program from the screenshot below:

Your screen should look like the screenshot below:

(N4)

Activities

8 Write a program that asks for and displays the title of a song and its position in the charts. Save it as Scratch Activity 8.

9 Write a program that asks for and displays your name and your age. Save it as Scratch Activity 9.

Designing a program

You need to be able to design a program. You can do this by using a structured diagram.

Structured diagrams can be used to explain just about any activity. Below is one that explains how to make a cup of tea.

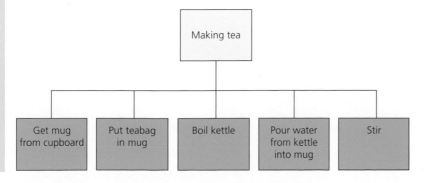

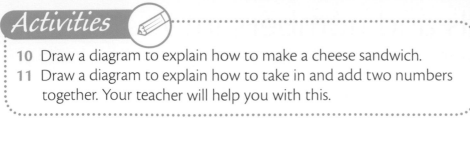

Activities

10 Draw a diagram to explain how to make a cheese sandwich.

11 Draw a diagram to explain how to take in and add two numbers together. Your teacher will help you with this.

Adding up numbers

Adding up numbers in Scratch is easy. You simply make the variables you need then use blocks in the *operators* window as to the right.

You are going to use the operator with the + sign as shown in the screenshot to the right.

Make the variables from the screenshot below:

Enter the program from the screenshot below:

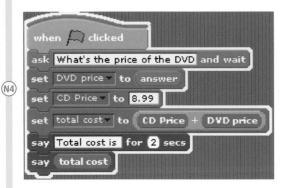

Your screen should look like the screenshot below:

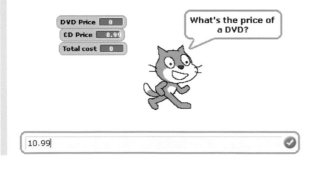

Activities

12 Write a program to add up the cost of two computer games and display the total.
- Draw a structure diagram for this program.
- Then write the program.

Save it as Scratch Activity 12.

13 Write a program to add up the cost of two films on DVD and display the average.
- Draw a structure diagram for this program.
- Then write the program.

Save it as Scratch Activity 13.

Activities

Super Task 1

Write a program to:

a) Enter the names and cost in pence of each of the following grocery items:

Honey	230
Salmon	198
Nuts	125
Tea	240
Eggs	175

b) Display the cost of each item and the total cost of all of the items.

The output from your program should look something like the screenshot below:

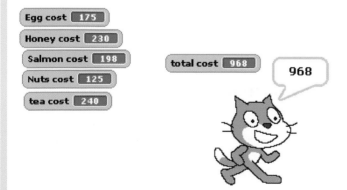

You need to complete a report for Super Task 1. The report should contain:
- a description of the task
- your structured diagram
- your test data.

You should ask your teacher to check:
- your report
- your coding
- your test run.

Using loops

Fixed loops

In programming we use loops to repeat actions over and over again.

Make a variable called *Name*.

Enter the program from the screenshot below:

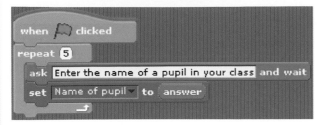

Your program should then ask you for the name of a pupil in your class five times.

Your screen should look something like the screenshot below:

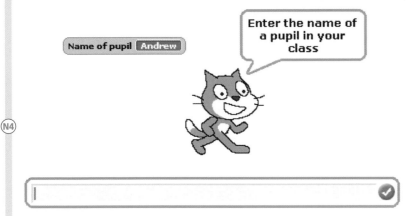

Now enter the program from the screenshot below on the left, which moves the sprite around in a circle by moving 6 × 60 degrees. The screenshot below on the right shows how your screen should look.

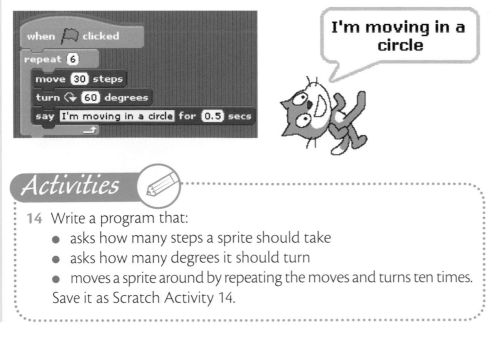

Activities

14 Write a program that:
- asks how many steps a sprite should take
- asks how many degrees it should turn
- moves a sprite around by repeating the moves and turns ten times.
Save it as Scratch Activity 14.

You can use the repeat loop to draw patterns on the screen.

This program uses a repeat loop and blocks from the *pen* window to draw a hexagon.

A hexagon has six sides and the angle of each of the turns is 60 degrees.

Enter the program from the screenshot below:

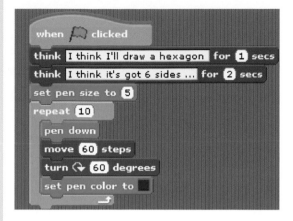

You might have to shrink the sprite down a bit so that it doesn't get in the way of the drawing! Your pattern should look like the screenshot below:

Activities

Super Task 2

Write a program that:
- asks the user to enter the number of sides in a drawing
- asks the user to enter the number of steps
- asks the user to enter the degrees of turn
- asks the user to enter the size of the pen
- asks the user to enter the colour of the pen as a number
- draws a pattern.

Test your program using this data

number of sides	8
number of steps	30
degrees of turn	45
size of pen	6
colour of pen	30

Your pattern should look like the screenshot below:

You need to complete a report for Super Task 2. The report should contain:
- a description of the task
- your structured diagram
- your test data.

You should ask your teacher to check:
- your report
- your coding
- your test run.

Arithmetical and comparator operators

You have already seen the arithmetic operators below. These are used for:

adding	+
subtraction	–
multiplying	*
division	/

The other operators you need to know about are the ones we use to make comparisons and these are shown in the screenshot below:

less than	<
equals	=
more than	>

Using *If*

You can use an *If* to get your program to make a decision. For example, your program can decide if a number is too big.

Make a variable called *Number of texts* then enter the program from the screenshot below:

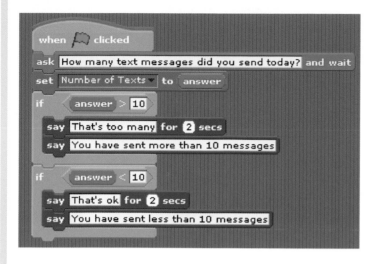

Your screen will look similar to the screenshot below:

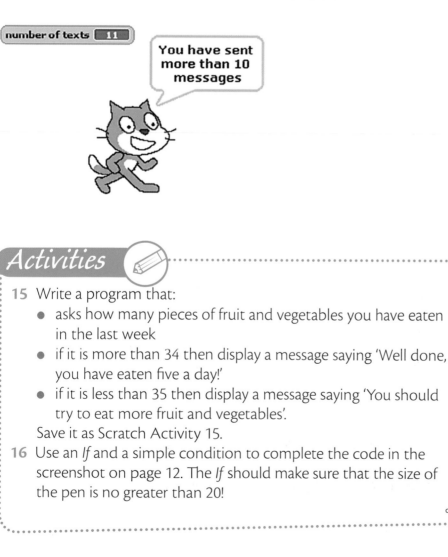

N4

Activities

15 Write a program that:
   - asks how many pieces of fruit and vegetables you have eaten in the last week
   - if it is more than 34 then display a message saying 'Well done, you have eaten five a day!'
   - if it is less than 35 then display a message saying 'You should try to eat more fruit and vegetables'.

   Save it as Scratch Activity 15.

16 Use an *If* and a simple condition to complete the code in the screenshot on page 12. The *If* should make sure that the size of the pen is no greater than 20!

⇨

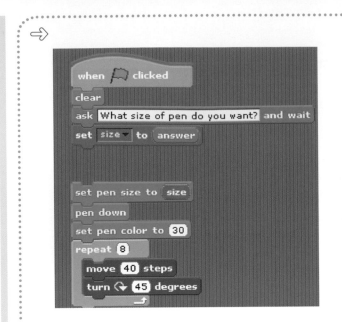

Your screen should look something like the screenshot below:

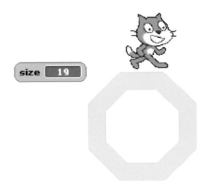

You can use an *If* to give the user a choice as shown in the screenshot below:

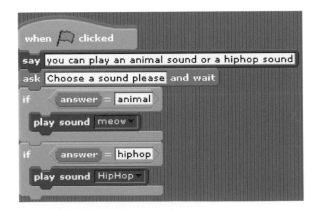

Enter the program shown above.
(You will need headphones to listen to the sound!)

17 Write a program that:
- offers the user a choice of sounds to play
- inputs the reader's choice
- then plays their choice
- and displays a suitable message.

Save it as Scratch Activity 17.

Using loops

Loops with simple conditions

You use loops to repeat actions until a condition is met.

In Scratch you use the *Repeat . . . until loop*.

The program in the screenshot below keeps asking for the cost of music downloads in pence until the total is greater than 800.

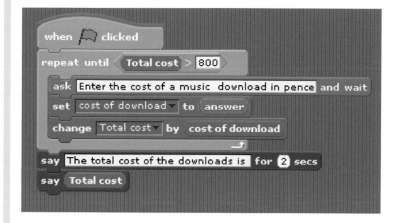

Enter the program above and test it out!

Your screen should look something like the screenshot below:

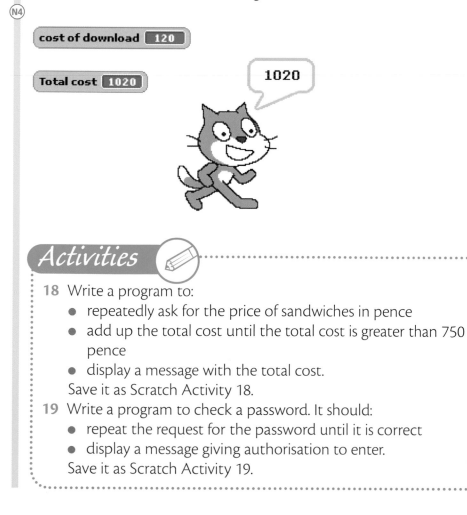

(N4)

Activities

18 Write a program to:
   - repeatedly ask for the price of sandwiches in pence
   - add up the total cost until the total cost is greater than 750 pence
   - display a message with the total cost.
   Save it as Scratch Activity 18.

19 Write a program to check a password. It should:
   - repeat the request for the password until it is correct
   - display a message giving authorisation to enter.
   Save it as Scratch Activity 19.

You can use repeat loops and conditions to make patterns.

Enter the program from the screenshot below:

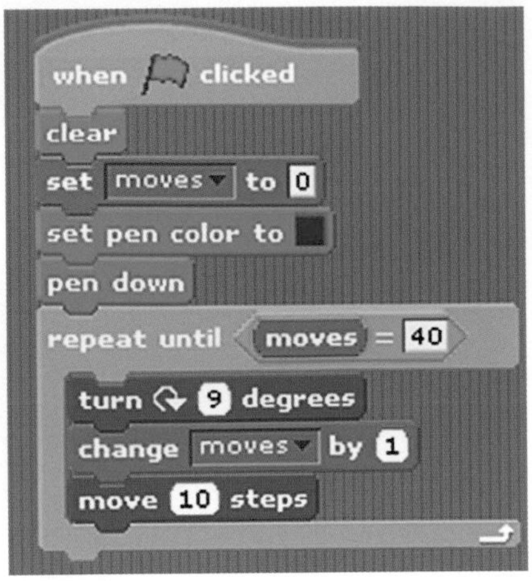

```
when  [flag]  clicked
clear
set  moves ▼  to  0
set pen color to  ■
pen down
repeat until  < moves = 40 >
    turn  ↻  9  degrees
    change  moves ▼  by  1
    move  10  steps
```

- It clears the screen
- then sets steps to 0
- sets the pen colour to red
- puts the pen down
- repeats until the number of moves = 40
- turns 9 degrees
- adds 1 to the number of moves
- moves 10 steps.

Your screen should look something like the screenshot below:

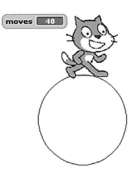

Activities

20 Write a program to draw a square. It will have:
- four sides, each side should be around 100 steps
- four 90-degree turns.

Your program should look like the screenshot below:

Activities

Super Task 3

Write a program to draw a pattern containing squares, octagons and a circle.

- Your program should use a variety of colours, sizes, sprites and movements to create an interesting colourful display.
- Your program should also ask the user to choose from a range of sounds available to play while the program is running.

You need to complete a report for Super Task 3. The report should contain:

- a description of the task
- your structured diagram
- your test data.

You should ask your teacher to check:

- your report
- your coding
- your test run.

Boolean variables

Boolean variables can be set to two values: True or false. They come in useful when, for example, we test the result of a condition.

In Visual Basic this is easy:

```
Dim target_reached as boolean = false ' target_reached is set to false
If total = > 200 Then
    target_reached = true ' target target_reached is set to true when the
    condition is met
End If
```

You can then use the Boolean variable as a control for another process:

```
If target_reached = true Then
    call Bonus_display
End If
```

In Scratch there is no Boolean variable and you have to use a workaround as shown in the screenshot below.

You could then use *target_reached* as a Boolean by using target_reached set to 1 as True and target_reached set to 0 as false.

But this is a workaround and it is rather awkward, though it does work!

Activities

21 Write a program that uses a Boolean (workaround) variable:
   - to check that the answer to each one of three quiz questions is correct
   - to add five points to the total score for a correct answer.

Using arrays

An array is a list of numbers or words. Each array has a name. This array is called *Name*.

Index	1	2	3	4
Name	Fred	Ted	Ed	Ned

Each array has an index. The index is used to count down (or up) the array.

So *Name(1)* is Fred, *Name(2)* is Ted and so on.

This array is called Prices.

Index	1	2	3	4
Prices	34.99	12.50	14.30	56.00

Here *Prices(1)* is 34.99, *Prices(2)* is 12.50 and so on.

Setting up and filling an array

The first thing you have to do is set up your array using the *Make a list* block in the *variables* menu as in the screenshot on the right.

`Make a list`

Call the list *Grocery Items*. It should appear on your screen. You might have to stretch it to make it bigger! You will need to set up a counter to count down the index as shown in the screenshot below:

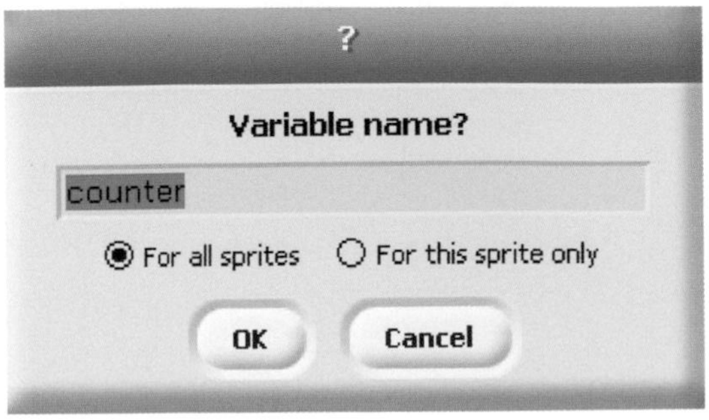

Activities

22 a) Set up a list called *Grocery Items* and a variable called *counter*, then enter the program in the screenshot below. It:

- sets the counter to 1
- asks for the grocery item
- adds it to the array
- adds 1 to the counter.

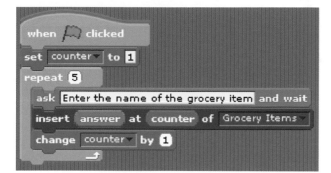

Your screen should look something like the screenshot below:

If you want to you can get a sprite to output the groceries!
Note: Scratch arrays can hold either *strings* or *numbers*.

b) Set up and fill an array to hold the prices of the grocery items. Your screen should look like the screenshot below:

⇨ Now add the scripts from the screenshot below to calculate the average cost:

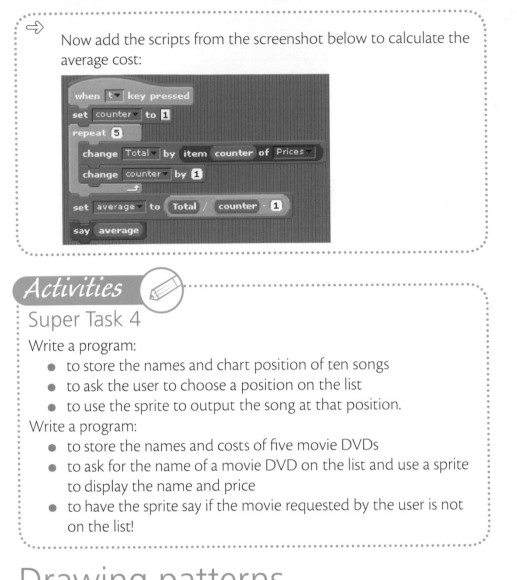

Activities

Super Task 4

Write a program:
- to store the names and chart position of ten songs
- to ask the user to choose a position on the list
- to use the sprite to output the song at that position.

Write a program:
- to store the names and costs of five movie DVDs
- to ask for the name of a movie DVD on the list and use a sprite to display the name and price
- to have the sprite say if the movie requested by the user is not on the list!

Drawing patterns

Scratch can be used to draw complex patterns and play sounds. A useful feature is the *random* function shown in the screenshot to the right, which selects random numbers from a range that you specify. This can be really useful when you want to move a sprite or a pen around the screen.

Enter the code from the screenshot below:

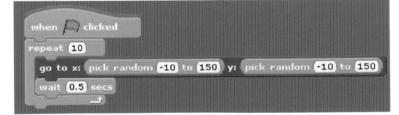

Now add the code from the screenshot below to draw the sprite's random path. You might want to shrink your sprite so that you can see the path it draws more clearly.

```
pen down
set pen color to ■
set pen size to 5
```

Activities

23 Write a program to move your sprite across the entire screen at random and draw a colourful path as it does so. Shrink your sprite to a small dot, then enter the code from the screenshot below and run it.

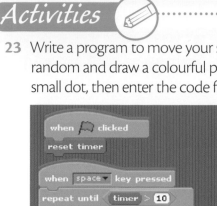

Your screen should look like the screenshot below:

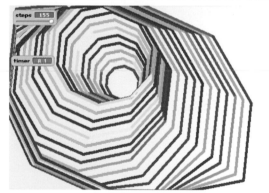

Activities

Super Task 5

Write a program.

- Create a pattern using a decagon.
- The decagon should increase its size as it moves around the screen until it reaches a maximum of 150 steps.
- It should then stop, play a sound and output a message using a sprite.
- It should use a timer to record the length of time it takes to make the pattern.
- If the pattern takes more than 20 seconds it should output a suitable message.

Developing Software using Visual Basic

Visual Basic introduction

Step 1 Getting started

Your teacher will help you open Visual Basic and make sure that the *standard* toolbar is showing by using the *view* and *toolbar* menus.

Now select Windows application and give it a name as shown in the screenshot below.

```
New Project                                                          [?] [X]

Templates:                                                          [::::] [::]

 ┌─ Visual Studio installed templates ──────────────────────────────────┐
 │   [VB]        [VB]        [C#/VB]      [My Movie]   [Screen]           │
 │                                                                        │
 │  Windows    Class Library  Console     My Movie    Screen Saver       │
 │  Application               Application Collecti... Starter Kit        │
 │                                                                        │
 │  My Templates                                                          │
 │                                                                        │
 │   [    ]                                                               │
 │  Search                                                                │
 │  Online Te...                                                          │
 │                                                                        │
 │                                                                        │
 │                                                                        │
 └────────────────────────────────────────────────────────────────────┘
 A project for creating an application with a Windows user interface

 Name:          My first project

                                            [  OK  ]      [ Cancel ]
```

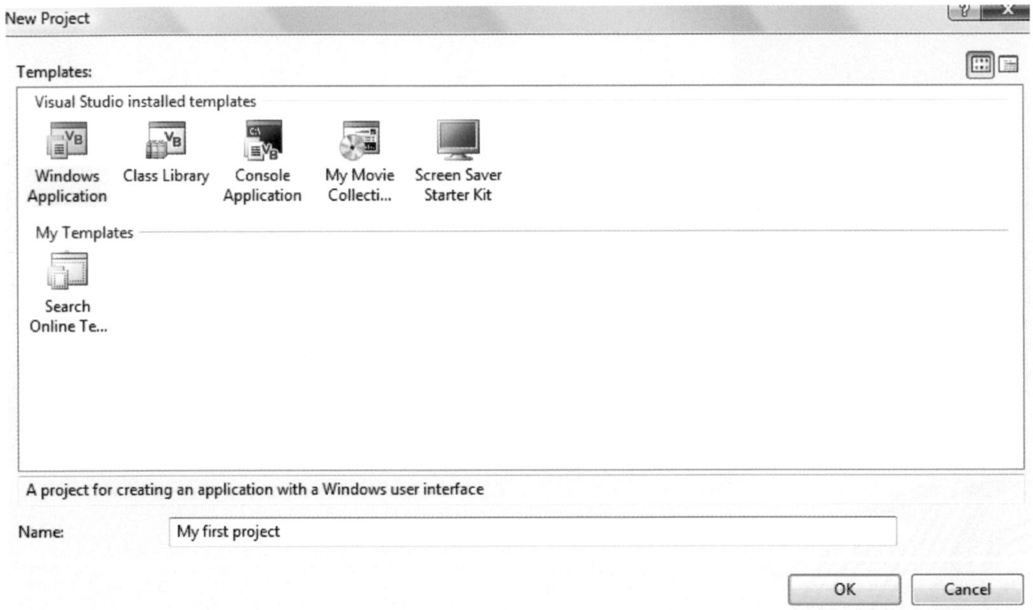

The *form* window will appear as shown in the screenshot below. This is where you will design your program.

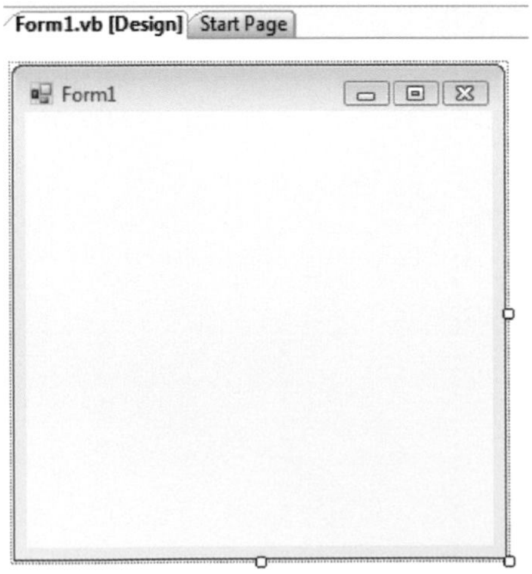

```
Form1.vb [Design]  Start Page

 ┌──────────────────────────────────────┐
 │ ■ Form1              [─] [□] [✕]      │
 ├──────────────────────────────────────┤
 │                                        │
 │                                        │
 │                                        │
 │                                        │
 │                                        │
 │                                        │
 │                                        │
 └──────────────────────────────────────┘
```

Step 2 Finding out about the toolbox

Your screen has a toolbox (see page 21) which is very important. Click on it to open it. It has lots of tools; don't worry, you are only going to use a few of them to start with. The ones you will mainly use will be:

- the *button* tool
- the *label* tool
- the *textbox* tool
- and, later on, the *listbox* tool.

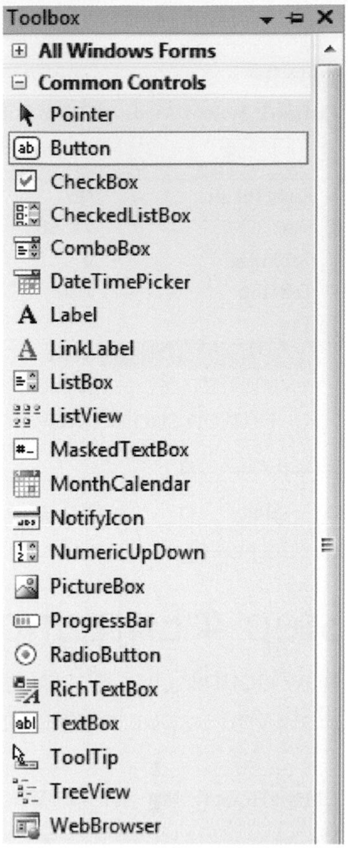

You will need to use the following icons:

New Project icon (that you have already seen)	
Open icon	
Save icon	

Step 3 Using a button

Open the toolbox and drag a button onto your form. You can change the shape of your button by dragging the handles. Your form should look something like the screenshot below:

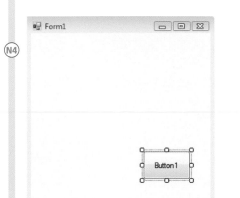

You should now change the text on the button to Start. To do this you need to go to the *properties* window, which is on the right-hand side of your screen.

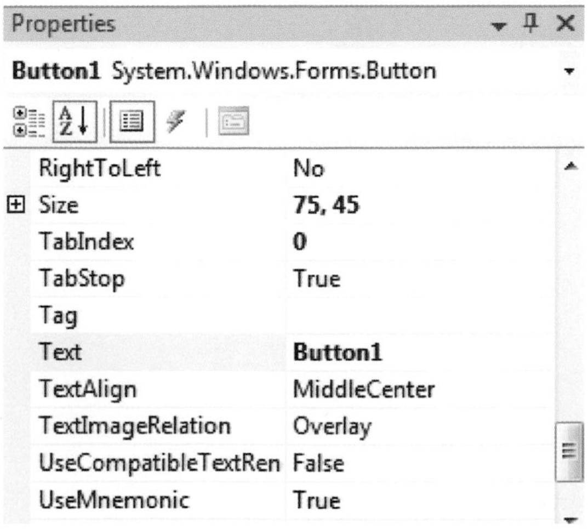

Properties

Button1 System.Windows.Forms.Button

RightToLeft	No
⊞ Size	75, 45
TabIndex	0
TabStop	True
Tag	
Text	**Button1**
TextAlign	MiddleCenter
TextImageRelation	Overlay
UseCompatibleTextRen	False
UseMnemonic	True

Toolbox

- ⊞ **All Windows Forms**
- ⊟ **Common Controls**
  - Pointer
  - Button
  - CheckBox
  - CheckedListBox
  - ComboBox
  - DateTimePicker
  - Label
  - LinkLabel
  - ListBox
  - ListView
  - MaskedTextBox
  - MonthCalendar
  - NotifyIcon
  - NumericUpDown
  - PictureBox
  - ProgressBar
  - RadioButton
  - RichTextBox
  - TextBox
  - ToolTip
  - TreeView
  - WebBrowser

Click on the text Button1 and change it to Start as on the screenshot below:

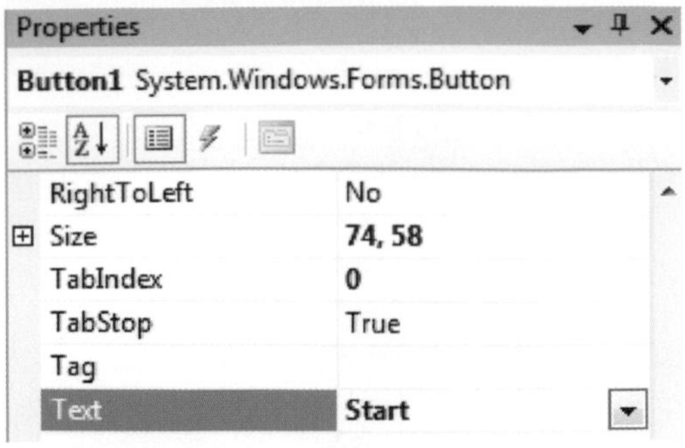

Your button should now look like the screenshot below:

Step 4 Entering your first program code

Now double click on your *start* button and the window will open to allow you to put in your program code. The code you will put in will be:

```
MsgBox("My first VB program by my name")
```

Be careful to type it in correctly, making sure you enter the brackets ( ) and the " ".

N4 Note: You should put in your own name!

This code will open up a message box on the screen and print the text in between the brackets and speech marks (" ") as shown in the screenshot below.

```
Public Class Form1

    Private Sub Button1_Click(ByVal sender As System

        MsgBox(" My first VB program by my name")

    End Sub
End Class
```

Step 5 Testing your program

Now test your program by clicking on the *run* icon at the top of the screen, which is shown in the screenshot to the right.

Now click on the *start* button and, if there are no errors, your screen will look like the screenshot below:

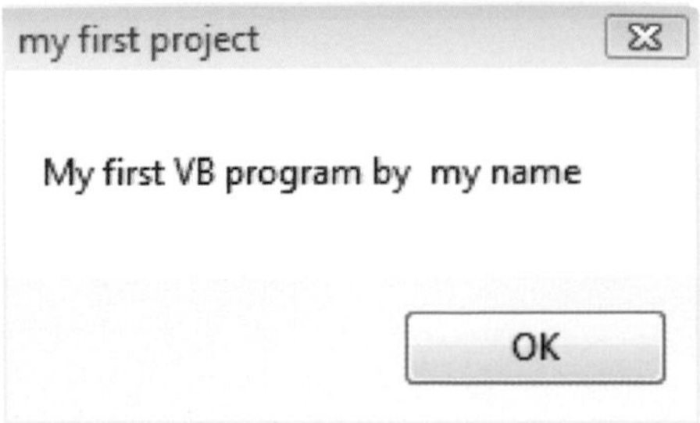

Click on OK and the message box will go away. Now stop your program running by clicking on the stop icon (see screenshot to the right) at the top of the screen.

Step 6 Saving your program

Now save your program by opening the *file* menu and selecting Save All as shown in the screenshot on the right:

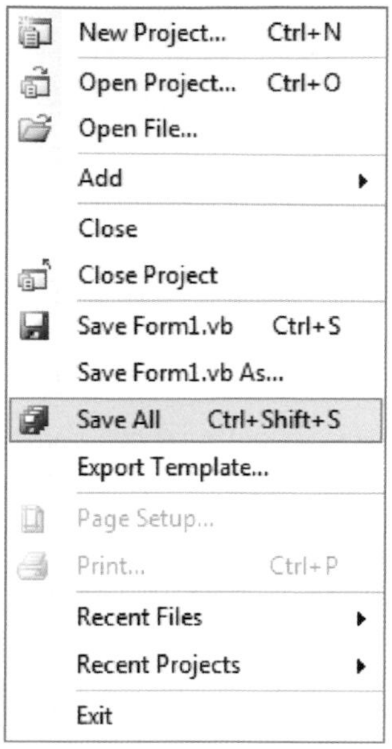

Now name your project *first project* and click on Save as shown in the screenshot below:

📄	New Project...	Ctrl+N
📄	Open Project...	Ctrl+O
📂	Open File...	
	Add	▶
	Close	
📄	Close Project	
💾	Save Form1.vb	Ctrl+S
	Save Form1.vb As...	
📄	**Save All**	**Ctrl+Shift+S**
	Export Template...	
📄	Page Setup...	
🖨	Print...	Ctrl+P
	Recent Files	▶
	Recent Projects	▶
	Exit	

Save Project

Name:	first project
Location:	C:\Users\ff\Documents\Visual Studio 2005\Projects
Solution Name:	first project ☑ Create directory for solution

Save   Cancel

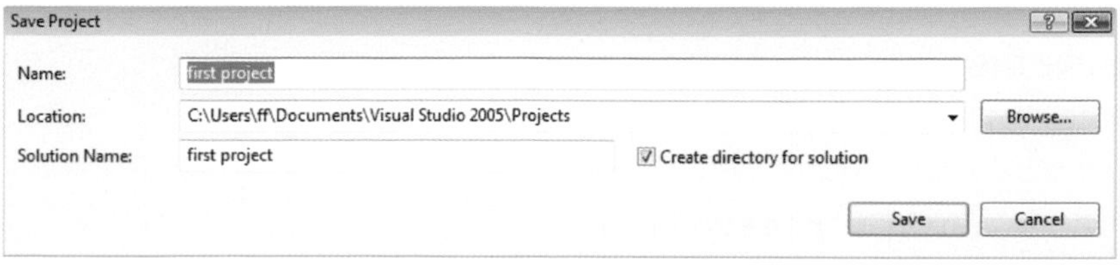

You have now completed your first VB project!

Activities ✏

1 Print your school name using a message box. Save it as Visual Basic Activity 1.
2 Print your address using a message box. Save it as Visual Basic Activity 2.
3 Print your favourite pop star's name using a message box. Save it as Visual Basic Activity 3.

(N4)

Step 7 Getting numbers into your program

In this section you are going to learn how to get whole numbers into your program. In Visual Basic we call a whole number an integer. To get a number in, we are going to use an input box that will appear on the screen. Input boxes are used to get data in from a user as shown in the screenshot below:

WindowsApplication1   ✕

enter a whole number please

OK

Cancel

14

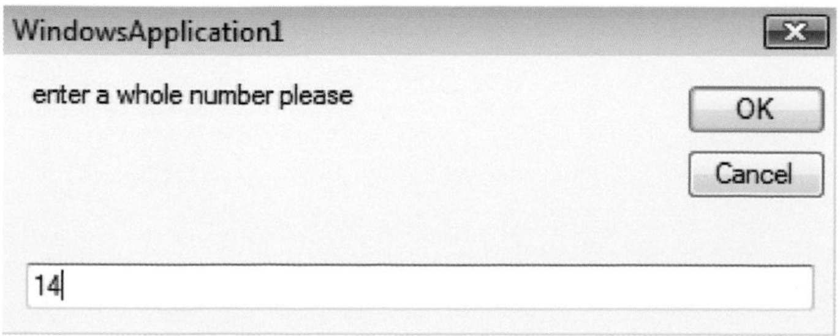

We will use the code:

```
Inputbox("Enter a whole number please")
```

But we will need to put the number that is entered into a box in the computer's memory. We call these boxes variables. So we will have to set up a box called *number* using this line of code:

```
Dim number As Integer
```

This sets up a box in the computer's memory called *number*.

Now you have to tell the computer to take the number from the input box and put it into the number box using this line of code:

```
number = Inputbox("Enter a whole number please")
```

We can then tell the computer to use a message box to put a message, and whatever is in the number box, on the screen using this line of code:

```
MsgBox("The number you entered was" & number)
```

Now let's get started by opening up a new form by following Step 1 again. This time call your new project *Integer example*. Now add a button and change its text to Start, following Step 3 on pages 21–22.

Now double click on the *start* button to open your *coding* window and enter your code. Your screen should look like the screenshot below:

```
Public Class Form1

    Private Sub Button1_Click(ByVal sender As System.Object, ByVal

        Dim number As Integer
        number = InputBox("enter a whole number please ")
        MsgBox("You entered the whole number " & number)

    End Sub
End Class
```

Test

Now test your program by clicking on the *run* icon. If there are no errors then the input box will ask you to enter a number and the message box will display the number on the screen as shown in the screenshot below.

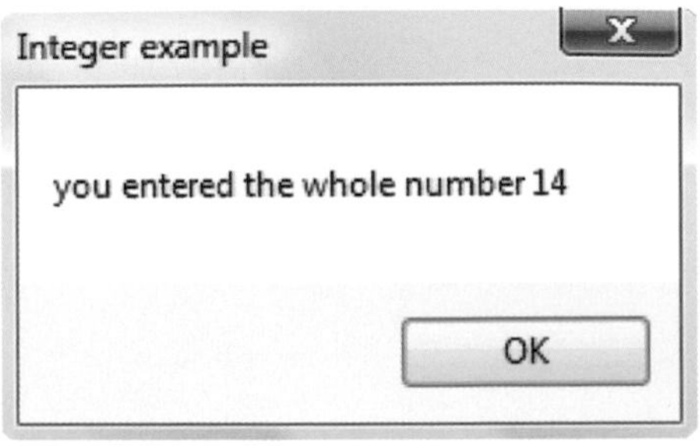

Don't forget to stop the program running by clicking on the *stop* icon.

Now save your project as *Integer example* by selecting Save All from the *file* menu as shown in the screenshot on the right.

New Project...	Ctrl+N	
Open Project...	Ctrl+O	
Open File...		
Add		▶
Close		
Close Project		
Save Form1.vb	Ctrl+S	
Save Form1.vb As...		
Save All	Ctrl+Shift+S	
Export Template...		
Page Setup...		
Print...	Ctrl+P	
Recent Files		▶
Recent Projects		▶
Exit		

Activities

4 Write a program that asks for and displays the number of people in your family. Save it as Visual Basic Activity 4.
5 Write a program that asks for and displays the number of hours you watch television each day. Save it as Visual Basic Activity 5.

Remember

Variables

Variables are boxes in the computer's memory that you use to store, for example, numbers or words.

So far you have only used a variable to hold a whole number like 1, 2, 3 and so on, but you can store decimal numbers, for example, 1.25, 2.34, 20.45.

Here are the different types of variables that you will use:

Type	Coding	What it can hold	Example
STRING	Dim Name as string	Letters	Fred
INTEGER	Dim Number as integer	Numbers without a fraction	14
SINGLE	Dim Decimal_number as single	Decimal numbers (fractions)	16.75

(N4)

Step 8 Getting words into your program

To get a name in you are going to use an input box which will appear on the screen. You will use the code:

```
InputBox("Enter a name please")
```

But we will need to put the name that is entered into a box in the computer's memory. We call these boxes variables. So we will have to set up a box called *name* using this line of code:

```
Dim name As String
```

Now you have to tell the computer to take the name from the input box and put it into the name box using this line of code:

```
name = InputBox("Enter a name please")
```

We can then tell the computer to use a message box to put a message, and whatever is in the name box, on the screen using this line of code:

```
MsgBox("The name you entered was" & name)
```

Now let's get started by opening up a new form by following Step 1 again. Just as you did for numbers, open up a new project and call it *Name example*.

Now add a button to your form and change its text to Start, just as you did in Step 3 on pages 21–22.

Your form should look like the screenshot below:

```
Public Class Form1

    Private Sub Button1_Click(ByVal sender As System.Object,

        Dim name As String

        name = InputBox(" enter a name please")

        MsgBox("The name you entered was " & name)

    End Sub
End Class
```

Now double click on the *start* button and enter the code for your program so that it looks like the screenshot below:

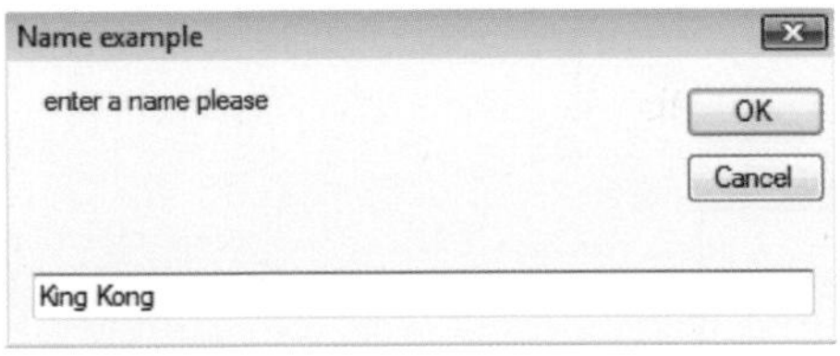

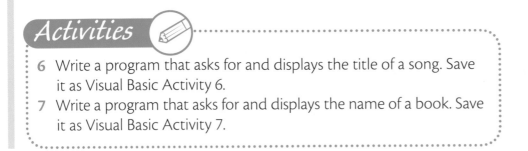

Test

Now test your program by clicking on the *run* icon. If there are no errors then the input box will ask you to enter a name and the message box will display the name on the screen as in the screenshot below.

Now save your project as *name example* by selecting Save All from the *file* menu.

Activities

6 Write a program that asks for and displays the title of a song. Save it as Visual Basic Activity 6.
7 Write a program that asks for and displays the name of a book. Save it as Visual Basic Activity 7.

Step 9 Getting words and numbers into your program

Now you are going to write a program that will input words and numbers and display them on the screen. Open a new project and call it *Words and numbers*. Put a start button on your form. Now enter the code that follows to input the name of a pop star and give them a rating number between 1 and 5.

```
Dim Pop_star_name As String
Dim rating As Integer
Pop_star_name = InputBox("Enter the name of a pop star please")
rating = InputBox("Give your pop star a rating between 1 and 5. 1 is the
best and 5 the worst.")
MsgBox("Your pop star you entered was " & Pop_star_name)
MsgBox("The rating you gave was " & rating)
```

Your coding should look like this:

```
Public Class Form1
    Private Sub Button1_Click(ByVal sender As System.Object, ByVal e As
    System.EventArgs) Handles Button1.Click
        Dim Pop_star_name As String
        Dim rating As Integer
        Pop_star_name = InputBox("Enter the name of a pop star please")
        rating = InputBox("Give your pop star a rating between 1 and 5. 1
        is the best and 5 the worst.")
        MsgBox("Your pop star you entered was " & Pop_star_name)
        MsgBox("The rating you gave was " & rating)
    End Sub
End Class
```

Note: If you want to use a variable name with two or more words, you have to use the underscore like this:

```
Pop_Star_Name
```

You can't use *Pop Star Name*, as Visual Basic won't accept spaces in a variable name.

Test

Now test your program using the *run* icon.

Don't forget to stop the program running by clicking on the *stop* icon. Save your program as *Names and numbers*.

Note: From now on you should place comments in your program explaining who wrote it, when it was written and what the program does.

```
' Program to ask for song and position in charts
' By Ali Mac
' May 2013
' Saved as 'Name and Age'
```

Note: You have to start a comment by using '.

Activities

8 Write a program that asks for and displays the title of a song and its position in the charts. Save it as Visual Basic Activity 8.
9 Write a program that asks for and displays your name and your age. Save it as Visual Basic Activity 9.

Step 10 Designing a program

You need to be able to design a program. You can do this by using a structured diagram. Structured diagrams can be used to explain just about any activity. Here is one that explains how to make a cup of tea.

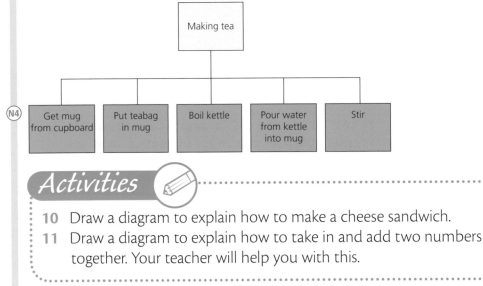

Activities

10 Draw a diagram to explain how to make a cheese sandwich.
11 Draw a diagram to explain how to take in and add two numbers together. Your teacher will help you with this.

Step 11 Adding up numbers

You are now going to write a program to add up some numbers.

Open a new project. Call it *Adding up*. On your form place a button and change its text to *Add numbers* as shown in the screenshot below.

Double click on the *Add numbers* button to open up the window for your coding.

First you need to set up the boxes (the variables) to store the numbers:

```
Dim cd_cost As Integer
Dim dvd_cost As Integer
Dim total_cost As Integer
```

Now you need to enter the code to input the costs:

```
cd_cost = InputBox("Enter the cost of a CD in pence please")
dvd_cost = InputBox("Enter the cost of a DVD in pence please")
```

Next add the code to add up the two costs to give the total cost:

```
total_cost = cd_cost + dvd_cost
```

Lastly, use a message box to display the total cost to the screen:

```
MsgBox("The total cost in pence = " & total_cost)
```

Your screen should now look like this:

```
Public Class Form1
    Private Sub Button1_Click(ByVal sender As System.Object, ByVal e As
    System.EventArgs) Handles Button1.Click
        Dim cd_cost As Integer
        Dim dvd_cost As Integer
        Dim total_cost As Integer
        cd_cost = InputBox("Enter the cost of a CD in pence please")
        dvd_cost = InputBox("Enter the cost of a DVD in pence please")
        total_cost = dvd_cost
        MsgBox("The total cost in pence = " & total_cost)
    End Sub
End Class
```

Now test your program using the *run* icon. Don't forget to stop the program running by clicking on the *stop* icon. Save your program as *adding up*.

Adding, subtracting, multiplying, dividing, power of

You have used the + sign for adding up. You need to know how to subtract, multiply and divide. Use this table to help you.

Adding	+
Subtracting	−
Multiplying	*
Dividing	/
Power of	^

Activities

12 Write a program to add up the cost of two computer games and display the total.
   - Draw a structure diagram for this program.
   - Then write the program.

   Save it as Visual Basic Activity 12.

13 Write a program to add up the cost of two films on DVD and display the total.
   - Draw a structure diagram for this program.
   - Then write the program.

   Save it as Visual Basic Activity 13.

Activities

Super Task 1

Write a program to:

a) Enter the names and cost in pence of each of the following grocery items:

Honey   230
Salmon 198
Nuts   125
Tea   240
Eggs   175

b) Display the total cost of all of the items.

c) Calculate and display your change from £10.

The output from your program should look something like the screenshot on the right:

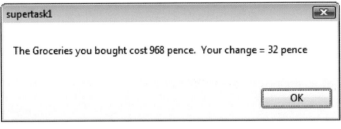

supertask1

The Groceries you bought cost 968 pence. Your change = 32 pence

OK

You need to complete a report for Super Task 1. The report should contain:
- a description of the task
- your structured diagram
- the test data you have been given (the list of groceries and costs).

You should ask your teacher to check:
- your report
- your coding
- your test run.

Step 12 Using a loop

In programming we use *loops* to repeat actions over and over again.

Open a new form as shown in the screenshot below.

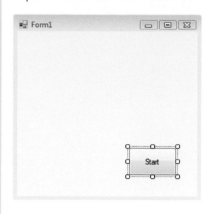

Place a start button on the form, click on the button and enter the coding below:

```
Dim counter As Integer
Dim name As String
For counter = 1 To 5
        name = Inputbox("Enter the name of a pupil in your class please")
     Msgbox("The name you entered was " & name)
Next
```

The program will go round the loop five times, taking in a name each time and displaying it in a message box.

Your form should look like this:

```
Public Class Form1
    Private Sub Button1_Click(ByVal sender As System.Object, ByVal e As
    System.EventArgs) Handles Button1.Click
        Dim counter As Integer
        Dim name As String
        For counter = 1 To 5
            name = InputBox("Enter the name of a pupil in your class please")
            MsgBox("The name you entered was " & name)
        Next
    End Sub
End Class
```

Now test your program using the *run* icon. Your program should ask you five times for the name of a pupil in your class then display it!

Don't forget to stop the program running by clicking on the *stop* icon.

Save your program as *For Next1*.

Step 13 Using a loop with a listbox

You use listboxes when you want to display lists of names or numbers, for example.

Open a new form and add a button. Change its text to read *Enter Names*.

Then add a list box. You will find it in your toolbox:

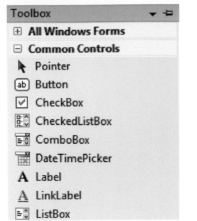

Go to the *properties* window and change the name of the listbox to *Names_list* as shown on the screenshot below.

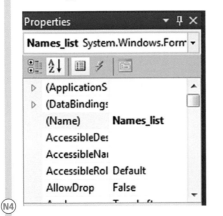

Your form should now look like the screenshot below:

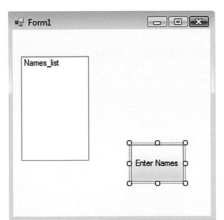

Now click on the *Enter Names* button and add this coding:

```
Public Class Form1
    Private Sub Button1_Click(ByVal sender As System.Object, ByVal e As
    System.EventArgs) Handles Button1.Click
        Dim counter As Integer
        Dim name As String
        For counter = 1 To 5
            name = InputBox("Enter the name of a pupil in your class please")
            Names_list.Items.Add(name)
        Next
    End Sub
End Class
```

Now test your program using the *run* icon.

Your program should ask you five times for the name of a pupil in your class then display it in the listbox as shown on the screenshot below.

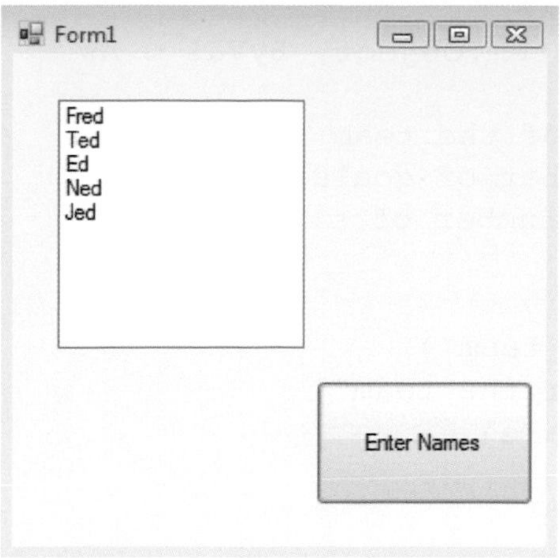

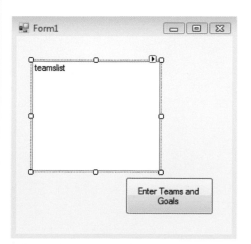

Don't forget to stop the program running by clicking on the *stop* icon. Save your program as *For Next listbox*.

Activities

14 Write a program to enter and display the names of five of your favourite pop stars.
   ● Draw a structure diagram for this program.
   ● Then write the program.
   Save it as Visual Basic Activity 14.

Step 14 Using a loop and a listbox to display names and numbers

Open a new form and add a button. Change its text to read *Enter Teams and Goals*.

Then add a listbox and change its name to *teamslist*.

Your form should now look like the screenshot below:

Now click on the *Enter Teams and Goals* button and add the coding below:

```
Public Class Form1
    Private Sub Button1_Click(ByVal sender As System.Object, ByVal e As
    System.EventArgs) Handles Button1.Click
        Dim team As String ' this holds the name of the team
        Dim goals As Integer ' this holds the number of goals
        Dim counter As Integer ' this counts the number of times around
        the loop
        For counter = 1 To 5
            team = InputBox("Enter the name of a team")
            goals = InputBox("Enter the goals for the team")
            teamslist.Items.Add(team & " " & goals)
        Next
    End Sub
End Class
```

Note: Ensure this time you have added comments to explain what is going on in your program.

Remember

Comments start with a '. For example:

' this holds the name of the team

Comments are coloured green!

Now test your program using the *run* icon.

Your form should look something like the screenshot below.

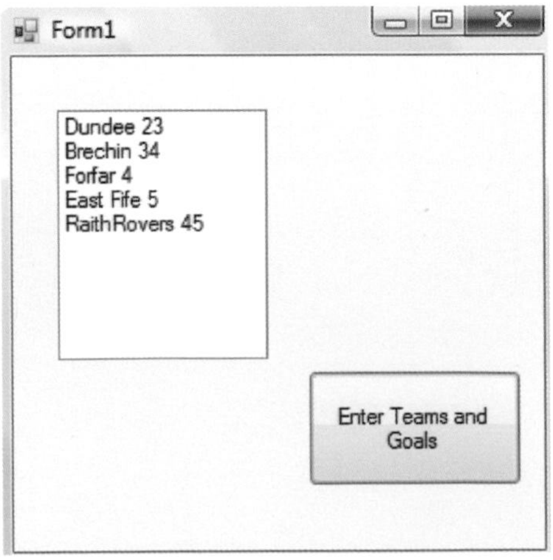

Form1

Dundee 23
Brechin 34
Forfar 4
East Fife 5
Raith Rovers 45

Enter Teams and
Goals

Don't forget to stop the program running by clicking on the stop icon.
Save your program as *Teams and Goals*.

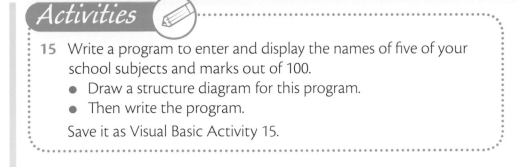

Activities

15 Write a program to enter and display the names of five of your
school subjects and marks out of 100.
- Draw a structure diagram for this program.
- Then write the program.
Save it as Visual Basic Activity 15.

Step 15 Adding up and working out an average

Open up your *Teams and Goals* program and make the changes below to calculate the average number of goals.

You need to set up a variable to hold the total goals and one to hold the average.

```
Dim Total_goals As Integer
Dim Average As Integer
```

Inside the loop add this coding to calculate the total:

```
Total_goals= Total_goals + Goals
```

Outside the loop add this coding to calculate the average:

```
Average = Total_goals/5
```

Use a message box to output the average by adding this code *outside the loop*:

```
MsgBox = ("The average = " & Average)
```

Your form should now look like this:

```
Public Class Form1
     Private Sub Button1_Click(ByVal sender As System.Object, ByVal e As
     System.EventArgs) Handles Button1.Click
          ' A program using a for next loop and a listbox
          ' By Name D Onut
          Dim Team As String ' this holds the name of the team
          Dim Goals As Integer ' this holds the number of goals
          Dim counter As Integer ' this counts the number of times around
          the loop
          Dim Total_goals As Integer
          Dim Average As Integer
          For counter = 1 To 5
               Team = InputBox("Enter the name of a team")
               Goals = InputBox("Enter the goals for the team ")
               teamslist.Items.Add(Team & " " & Goals)
               Total_goals = Total_goals + Goals
          Next
          Average = Total_goals / 5
          MsgBox("The average = " & Average)
     End Sub
End Class
```

Now test your program using the *run* icon.

N4 Your output should look something like the screenshots below:

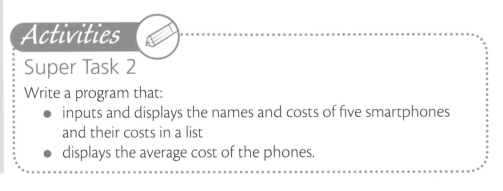

Don't forget to stop the program running by clicking on the stop icon.
Save your program as *Teams and Goals Average*.

Activities

Super Task 2

Write a program that:

- inputs and displays the names and costs of five smartphones and their costs in a list
- displays the average cost of the phones.

You need to complete a report for Super Task 2. The report should contain:
- a description of the task
- your structured diagram
- your test data.

You should ask your teacher to check:
- your report
- your coding
- your test run.

Using textboxes

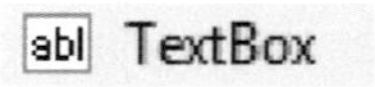

So far when we have been inputting data we have used an input box. You can also use a textbox to enter data. Let's start with a simple example. Open a new form and place a button on it. Change the button's text to *Get message* as shown in the screenshot on the right.

abl **TextBox**

Next go to your toolbox and place a textbox on your form. You are now going to give your textbox a suitable name using the *properties* window. Scroll up the *properties* window till you see the Name property. Now change it from *TextBox1* to *Read_number*.

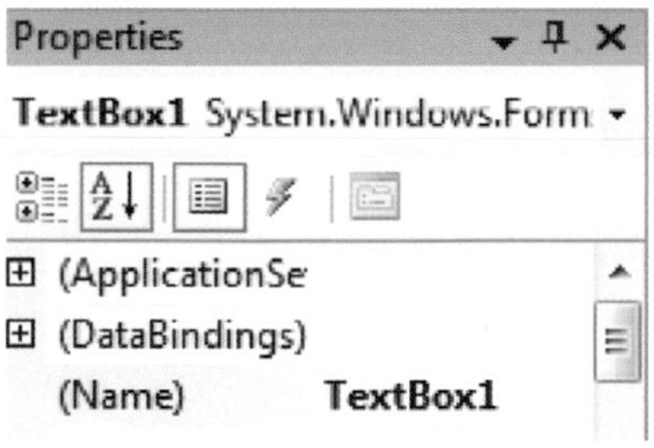

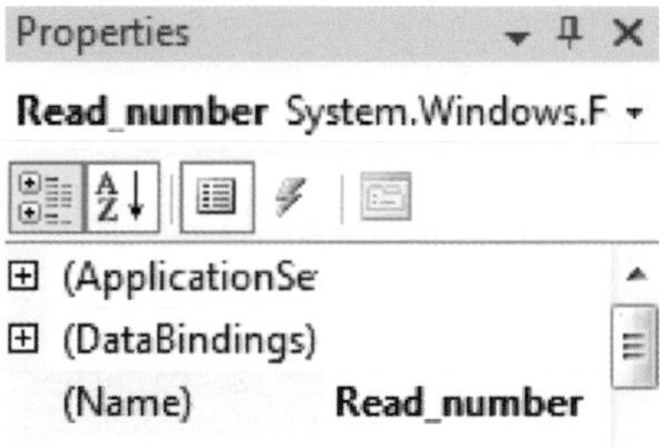

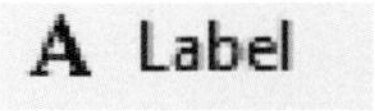

Now you need to add a label so that you know what the textbox is for. Go to your toolbox and drag a label onto your form and then change its text to read *Enter number*.

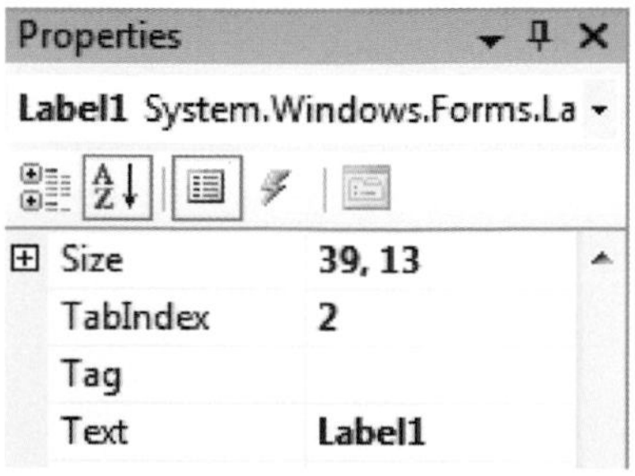

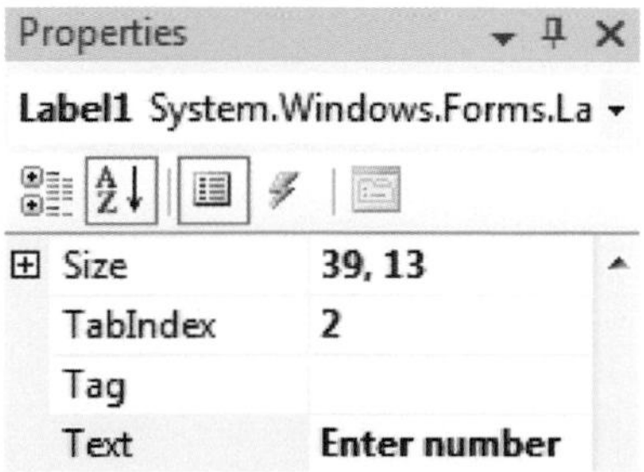

A Label

Your form should look something like the screenshot below:

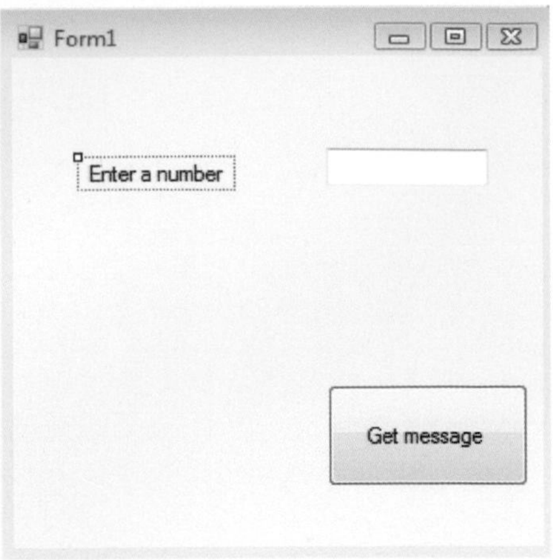

Now to enter the coding click on the *Get message* button, or click on the *form tab*.

Enter the coding below:

```
Dim number As Integer
number = Read_number.Text
MsgBox("The number you entered was " & number)
```

(N4)

Your coding should look like this:

```
Public Class Form1
    Private Sub Button1_Click(ByVal sender As System.Object, ByVal e As
    System.EventArgs) Handles Button1.Click
        Dim number As Integer
        number = Read_number.Text
        MsgBox("The number you entered was " & number)
    End Sub
End Class
```

Something is missing. Can you guess what it is? It is the comment lines.
● Add your own details at the start, for example:

```
' Program to XXXXXXXXX
' By XXXXXX
' Date XXXXX
' Saved as XXXXXXXX
```

- Add a few comment lines explaining what your program does.
- Test your program using the *run* icon.

Your form should look something like the screenshot below:

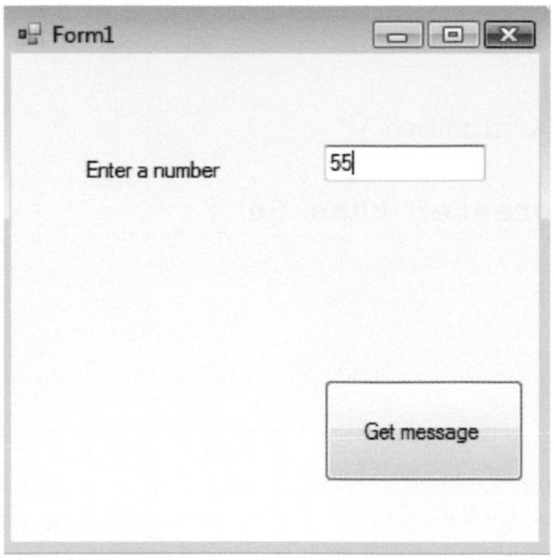

When you press the *Get message* button a message box like the one in the screenshot below should appear:

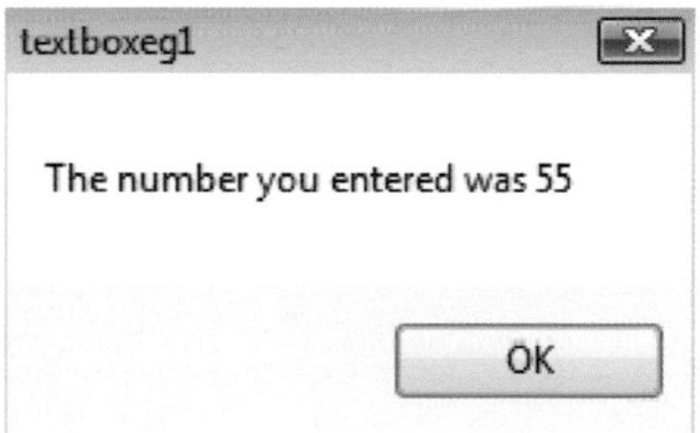

Don't forget to stop the program running by clicking on the *stop* icon.

Save your program as *textboxeg1*.

Note: Textboxes can also be used to display data that is used inside the program. You will see this later when we use textboxes to display numbers.

Using a textbox and an *If*

You can use an *If* to get your program to make a decision. For example, your program can decide if a number is too big.

Open the program *textboxeg1* you just completed. Add the coding below:

```
If number > 50 Then
     MsgBox("The number you entered was greater than 50")
End If
```

Your coding should now look like this:

```
Public Class Form1
    Private Sub Button1_Click(ByVal sender As System.Object, ByVal e As
    System.EventArgs) Handles Button1.Click
            Dim number As Integer
            number = Read_number.Text
            MsgBox("The number you entered was " & number)
            If number > 50 Then
               MsgBox("The number you entered was greater than 50")
          End If
      End Sub
  End Class
```

Now test your program using the *run* icon. Enter any number greater than 50, for example 55. When you press the *Get message* button a message box like this should appear:

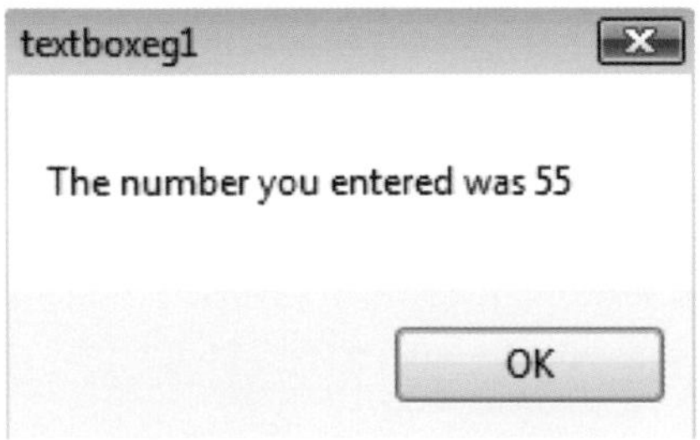

textboxeg1

The number you entered was 55

OK

When you click on the *OK* button another message box like this should appear:

textboxeg1

The number you entered was greater than 50

OK

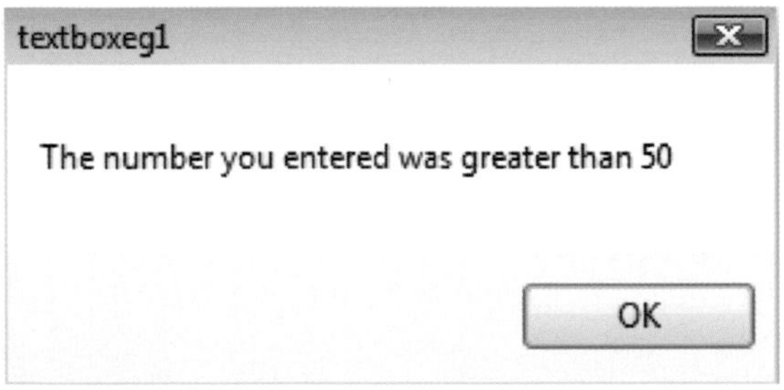

Don't forget to stop the program running by clicking on the *stop* icon.

Save your program as *Ifexample1*.

You used > to check if something was *greater than* something else. You need to know all the operators used for making comparisons:

Greater than	>
Less than	<
Equals	=
Does not equal	<>

Activities

16 Write a program that asks for the cost of a laptop computer. If the cost is greater than 200 then a suitable message should be output. Save your program as Visual Basic Activity 16.

17 Write a program to check a password. If the password is not correct then a message should be displayed refusing authorisation.
Save your program as Visual Basic Activity 17.

Activities

Super Task 3

Write a program that:

- takes in the names and marks out of 100 for 10 pupils
- displays the names and marks
- counts up how many pass (the pass mark is 50)
- displays the number of passes.

You need to complete a report for Super Task 3. The report should contain:

- a description of the task
- your structured diagram
- your test data.

You should ask your teacher to check:

- your report
- your coding
- your test run

Formatting numbers

You will need to change the way that numbers appear on your screen in some programs. Check out this example:

Open up a form and add a button with the text *Format a number* and three text boxes, each with a label as shown in the screenshot below:

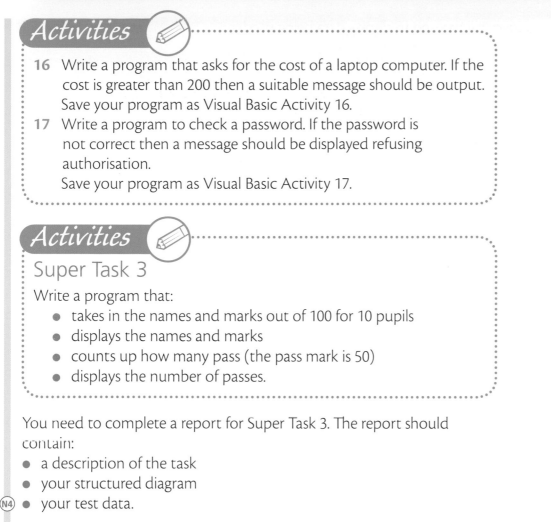

The textboxes in this program will be used to display data being used in the program.

Click on the button and enter the following text:

```
Dim number As Single
number = 45.6789
TextBox1.Text = Format(number, "standard")
TextBox2.Text = Format(number, "currency")
TextBox3.Text = Format(number, "general number")
MsgBox("The total cost is " & Format(number, "standard"))
MsgBox("The total cost is " & Format(number, "currency"))
MsgBox("The total cost is " & Format(number, "general number"))
```

Now test the program. It should look like the screenshot below:

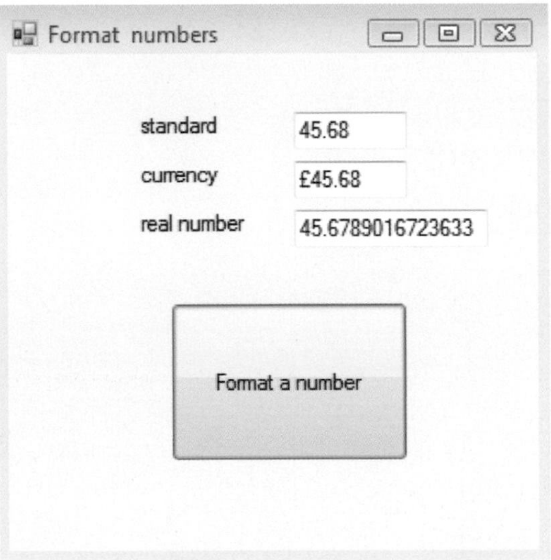

Remember

Formatting numbers

Format(number, "standard")	gives a number to two decimal places	45.68
Format(number, "currency")	gives a £ sign	£45.68
Format(number, "general number")	gives a number with lots of decimal places	45.67890167

Controlling a loop

You have used fixed loops to get your programs to repeat actions, for example:

```
Dim counter As Integer
For counter = 1 To 5
    ListBox1.Items.Add("My High School")
Next
```

This code will repeat the words *My High School* five times in a listbox as shown in the screenshot below.

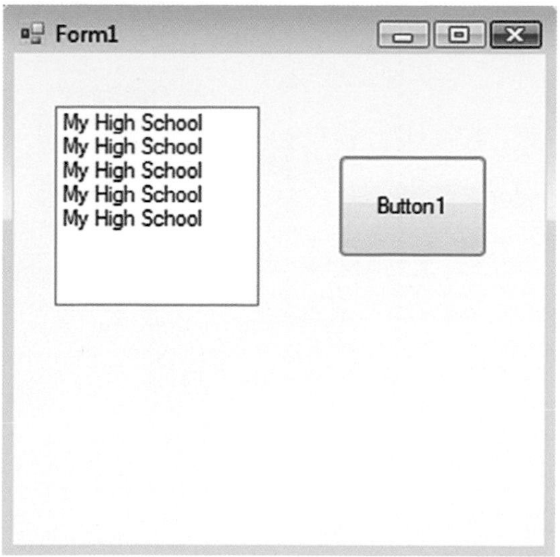

Now you are going to use a variable to let the user decide how many times the program will go round the loop.

Open a new project, add a *start* button then add the coding below:

(N4)

```
' Program to XXXXXXXXX
' By XXXXXX
' Date XXXXX
' Saved as XXXXXXXX
Dim number As Integer
Dim price As Integer
Dim total As Integer
Dim counter As Integer
price = InputBox("Enter the price of a computer game in pounds") ' this
takes in the price set by the user
number = InputBox("Enter the number of games you want to buy")
For counter = 1 To number ' uses the number variable to control the loop '
this takes in the number of games the user wants
total = total + price ' adds a price to the total each time round the loop
Next
    MsgBox("The total cost of your games is £" & total) ' this displays
    the total
```

This program uses the variable *number* to control the number of times round the *for…next loop*.

Test your program then save it as *Control Loop*.

Activities

18 Write a program that:
   a) asks for the number of pens a pupil wants
   b) asks for the price of a pen
   c) displays the total costs of the pens.
   Save your program as Visual Basic Activity 18.

19 Write a program that:
   a) asks for the number of books that a school wants to order
   b) asks for the price of a book
   c) displays the total costs of the books.
   Save your program as Visual Basic Activity 19.

Conditional loops

So far you have used *For…Next* loops to repeat actions in your programs.

Now you are going to use loops that are controlled by using conditions (conditional loops).

You are going to use *Do…loop until*.

Using *Do…loop until*

This program will ask the user to enter a number and then adds up the total until the total is greater than 100. The program will display the total as it goes along.

Pseudocode

1   Initialise

2   Loop enter numbers until total is greater than 100

1.1 setup number as an integer

1.2 setup total as an integer

2.1 start loop
       2.1 prompt for number
       2.2 input number
       2.3 add number to total
       2.4 display total

2.5 until total is greater than 100

****

Now:
● Open a new project.
● Add a start button.
● Add a textbox to your form.

- Change the textbox's name to output_total as shown in the screenshot below.

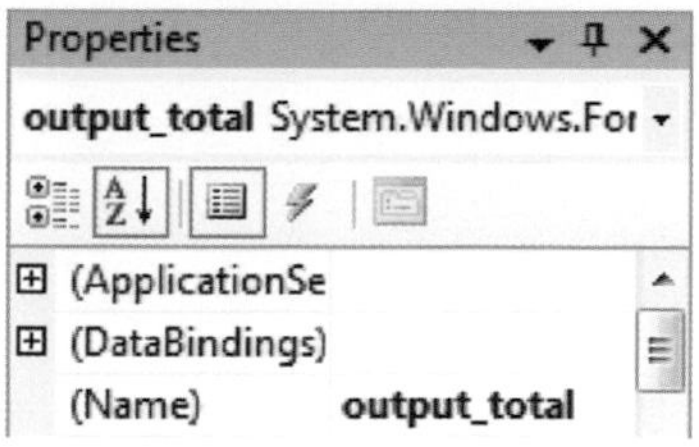

Now add a *label* to explain what the textbox is used for as shown in the screenshot below.

Your form should now look like the screenshot below:

Now click on your *start* button and add the following code:

```
Dim number As Integer
Dim total As Integer
Do
     number = InputBox("Enter a number please ")
     total = total + number ' adds a number to the total
     output_total.Text = total ' displays the total in the textbox
Loop Until total > 100 ' sets the condition: a total greater than 100
```

Your program should keep on asking for a number and changing the running total until it is greater than 100 as in the screenshot below.

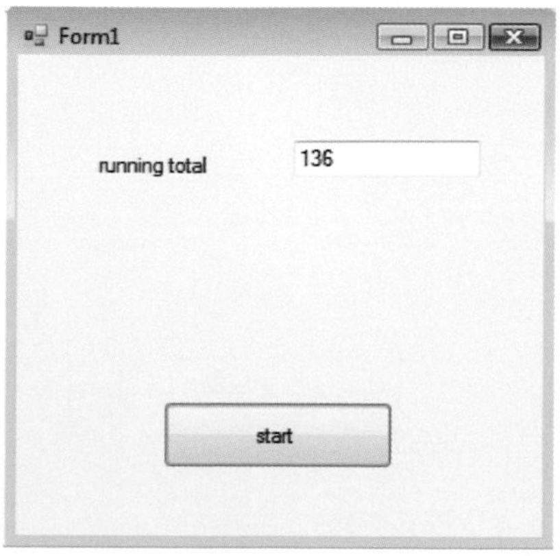

Save your program as *Do loop until example*.

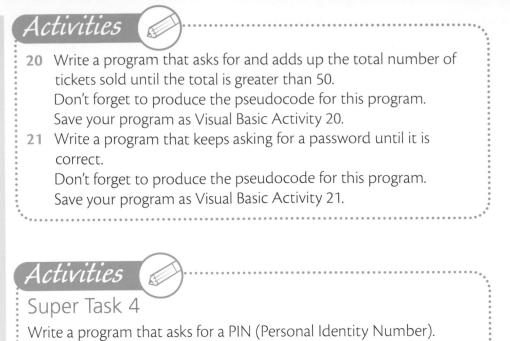

Activities

20 Write a program that asks for and adds up the total number of tickets sold until the total is greater than 50.
   Don't forget to produce the pseudocode for this program.
   Save your program as Visual Basic Activity 20.
21 Write a program that keeps asking for a password until it is correct.
   Don't forget to produce the pseudocode for this program.
   Save your program as Visual Basic Activity 21.

Activities

Super Task 4

Write a program that asks for a PIN (Personal Identity Number).
- If the PIN entered is '4848' then a 'correct' message should be displayed.
- If the PIN entered is not '4848' then an error message should be displayed and the user should be asked to enter the PIN again.
- The program should repeat this process until the correct PIN is entered.

You need to complete a report for Super Task 4. The report should contain:
- a description of the task
- your structured diagram
- your test data.

You should ask your teacher to check:
- your report
- your coding
- your test run.

You have now completed the National 4 level programming and you should now move to National 5 level.

Designing a program

At National 4 level you used structured diagrams to design your program.

At National 5 level you will use pseudocode to produce your designs. Pseudocode is a text-based method of designing a program that uses a language that is half-way between ordinary language and programming code.

You will use pseudocode to break down the problem you are given into ever smaller steps until you can code it.

Example

Problem

Write a program to:

- take in the cost of two laptops
- calculate the total cost including VAT
- output the total cost.

Pseudocode

1   Take in costs

2   Calculate total cost

3   Display total cost

1.1 prompt for cost of first laptop

1.2 input cost of first laptop

1.3 prompt for cost of second laptop

1.4 input cost of second laptop

2.1 calculate total cost as laptop1cost + laptop2cost

2.2 calculate VAT

2.3 add VAT to total cost

3.1 Display message

3.2 Display total cost

Activities

22 Open a Word file and write the pseudocode for a program that:
- takes in the cost of a mobile phone
- adds postage of £5.00 if the cost is less than £70
- displays the final cost.

You don't have to write the program, just the pseudocode. Save it as Visual Basic Activity 22.

Conditional loops

So far you have used *For . . . Next* loops to repeat actions in your programs. Now you are going to use loops that are controlled by using conditions.

You are going to use *Do . . . loop until* and *Do while . . . Loop*.

Using *Do . . . loop until* with a complex condition

This program will ask the user to enter a number, then adds up the total until the total is greater than 100 and less than 200. The program will display the total as it goes along.

Pseudocode

1. Initialise

2. Loop enter numbers until total is greater than 100

1.1 setup number as an integer

1.2 setup total as an integer

2.1 start loop

    2.1 prompt for number
    2.2 input number
    2.3 add number to total
    2.4 display total

2.5 until total is greater than 100 and less than 200

****

Open your saved *Do…loop until example.*

Now add the following complex condition to the end of the loop:

```
Loop Until total > 100 and total < 200 ' This is a complex condition
```

Your code should now look like this:

```
Dim number As Integer
Dim total As Integer
Do
      number = InputBox("Enter a number please ")
      total = total + number ' adds a number to the total
      output_total.Text = total ' displays the total in the textbox
Loop Until total > 100 and total < 200 ' This is a complex condition
```

Your program should keep on asking for a number and changing the running total until it is greater than 100 and less than 200 as in the screenshot below.

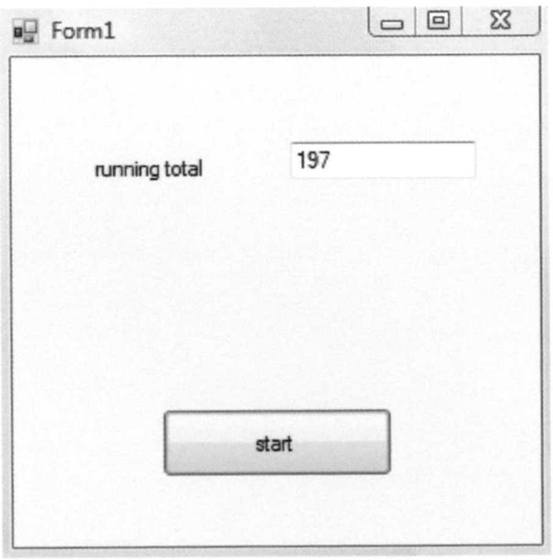

Save your program as *Do loop until example.*

Activities

23 Write a program that asks for and adds up the total number of tickets sold until the total is greater than 50 and less than 80. Don't forget to produce the pseudocode for this program. Save your program as Visual Basic Activity 23.

Using a *Do while... loop*

When you used the *Do...loop until*, the condition was at the end of the loop:

```
Do
     number = InputBox("Enter a number please ")
     total = total + number
     output_total.Text = total
Loop Until total > 100 and total <200 ' the condition is at the end of the
loop
```

When you use a *Do while ... loop* the condition is at the start of a loop:

```
Do While mark < 0
     mark= InputBox("Out of range, please enter a mark greater than 0")
Loop
```

This coding is using the *Do while...loop* to check that a mark being entered is greater than 0, a simple condition!

You will now write a program that will check that marks being entered are greater than −1 and less than 101. This is a complex condition with two parts to the condition: *greater than −1 and less than 101*.

● Start a new project.
● Add a button and change its text to *Average 5 Marks*.
● Add a textbox to hold the total of the five marks. Change its name to *Total_marks*. Give it a label with the same text.
● Add another textbox to hold the average mark. Change its name to *Average_mark*. Give it a label with the same name.

Your form should now look similar to the screenshot below:

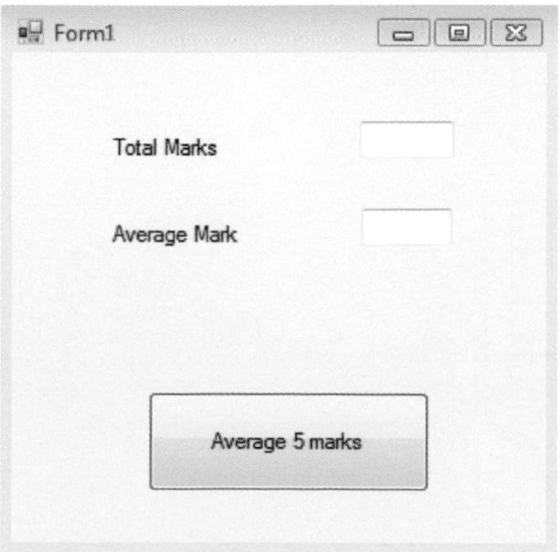

Now add the following code to your button:

```
' Program to XXXXXXXXX
' By XXXXXX
' Date XXXXX
' Saved as XXXXXXXX
Dim mark As Integer
Dim counter As Integer
Dim total As Integer
Dim average As Single ' note this can store numbers with decimal points
   For counter = 1 To 5
     mark = InputBox("Enter a mark between 0 and 100 ")
        Do While mark < 0 Or mark > 100 ' this holds a complex condition
           mark = InputBox("Out of range. Please enter a mark between 0 and
           100 ") ' this asks for another mark within the range
Loop
total = total + mark ' this adds up the marks using a running total
Total_marks.Text = total ' this puts the total into the Total_marks box
Next
   average = total / 5
   Average_mark.Text = average ' this puts the average into the Average
   _marks box
```

Test data

Now test your program by putting in a range of numbers that check whether or not marks below 0 or above 100 will be accepted.

You should include the numbers −1 and 101 as part of your test data.

Activities

24 Open a Word file and copy and complete this test data table:

Normal Test Data	Expected Result	Actual Result
23	mark accepted	
48	mark accepted	
75		
93		
Extreme Test Data	**Expected Result**	**Actual Result**
100	mark accepted	
101		
0		
−1	out of range	
Exceptional Test Data	**Expected Result**	**Actual Result**
2134	out of range	
897		
345.78		

If you enter a number that is out of range, you should get an error message as shown in the screenshot below:

DoWhile2

out of range. Please enter a mark between 0 and 100

OK

Cancel

Once you have entered five valid numbers, your form should look something like the screenshot below:

Form1

Total Marks   315

Average Mark   63

Average 5 marks

Save your program as *Do while example.*

Activities

25 Write a program that:
- asks the user to enter the cost of five different DVD movies.
- the maximum cost should be 14.99 and the minimum 5.50.
- calculates and displays the average cost of a DVD.

Save it as Visual Basic Activity 25.

You must:
- produce the pseudocode for this program
- produce a test data table for this program and complete it as you test the program.

Complex conditions

In the *Do while…* example above, you used a complex condition to check whether the mark was between 0 and 100.

When you use complex conditions you use one of the following operators: AND, OR, NOT

Operator	What it does
AND	Using *AND* joins two conditions together, for example: *If name ="Fred" and ID = "Fr1234" then…* both conditions must be met before the *If* is satisfied.
OR	Using an *OR* means that only one of the conditions needs to be met, for example: *If price < 0 OR price > 30 then…*
NOT	Using *NOT* negates a result for example: *IF NOT (number = 50) then…* If the conditional expression is false, then the result is true. If the conditional expression is true, then the result is false.

Activities

26 Write a program that:
   - asks the user for their customer number
   - gives an acceptance message if their customer number is greater than 0 and less than 1000.

   You must produce the pseudocode for this program.

   Save it as Visual Basic Activity 26.

If…then…else

You can use *If…then…else* to let your program decide two options. Enter the simple example below that checks a PIN number using a start button:

```
Dim pin_number As Integer
pin_number = 1234
    If pin_number = InputBox("Enter your PIN number please ") Then
    MsgBox("correct")
    Else : MsgBox("Wrong PIN number")
End If
```

ifthenelse	☒
wrong PIN number	
OK	

Activities

27 Write a program that checks the name of your favourite pop star. If the wrong name is entered then the program should display a suitable error message.

   Save it as Visual Basic Activity 27.

If...then...elseif...elseif...else end if

You can use *If ... then ... elseif ... elseif ... else end if* to allow your program to select between a range of options.

Try out this simple example:

```
Dim name As String
Dim comment As String
name = InputBox("Enter a name")
    If name = "Jack" Then
        comment = "Hi Jack"
    ElseIf name = "Mack" Then
        comment = "Hi Mack"
    ElseIf name = "Ed" Then
        comment = "Hi Ed"
    Else
        comment = "Who are you?"
    End If
    MsgBox(comment)
```

An alternative way of checking a multiple choice is to use a *CASE*:

```
Dim name As String
name = InputBox("Enter a name")
Select Case name
    Case Is = "Jack"
        MsgBox("Hi Jack")
    Case Is = "Mack"
        MsgBox("Hi Mack")
    Case Else
        MsgBox("Who are you?")
End Select
```

Activities

Super Task 5

Write a program to process five pupils' exam marks. The program should:

- take in five pupils' names and exam marks
- display each pupil's name, mark and their grade.

The grades must be awarded as follows:

Marks out of 100	Award
70–100	A
60–69	B
50–59	C
<50	D

You should supply your own test data table designed to make sure that the grading is done accurately.

You need to complete a report for Super Task 5. The report should contain:
- a description of the task
- your pseudocode
- a table with test data that you have produced.

You should ask your teacher to check:
- your report
- your coding
- your test run and test data table.

Using checkboxes

Checkboxes are an easy way to enter a user's selections into your form. Let's look at this example that uses checkboxes to make up a pizza:
- Start a new project.
- Add a button and change its text to *Show toppings chosen.*
- Add three checkboxes within and change each of their texts in turn to *Peppers, Cheese* and *Mushrooms.*
- Add labels to each checkbox with the text *Peppers, Cheese* and *Mushrooms.*
- Add a listbox and change its name to *Pizza.* Give it a label *Pizza toppings.*

Your form should look like this:

Now click on the button and add the following code:

```
If CheckBox1.Checked = True Then
    Pizza.Items.Add(CheckBox1.Text)
End If
If CheckBox2.Checked = True Then
    Pizza.Items.Add(CheckBox2.Text)
End If
If CheckBox2.Checked = True Then
    Pizza.Items.Add(CheckBox3.Text)
End If
```

This adds the text attached to the checkbox into the listbox if the checkbox is ticked.

Test your program. Your form should look something like the screenshot below:

28 Write a program that:
- uses checkboxes to select four smartphones from a list of five
- stores their costs in an array
- displays the individual costs and total cost of the four phones.

Nofia v6	£60.99
Blueberry Super5	£90.00
BearPhone V3	£20.34
Gibber V5	£50.89
TeaMobil	£67.45

Save it as Visual Basic Activity 28.

Combobox

A combobox provides the user with a dropdown menu from which they can choose *one* item.

Comboboxes are useful when you want to give the user a limited choice.

The user's selection from a combobox is read in as text.

Here a combobox is being used to find out the number of items being ordered and checkboxes to get the customer's choice of item.

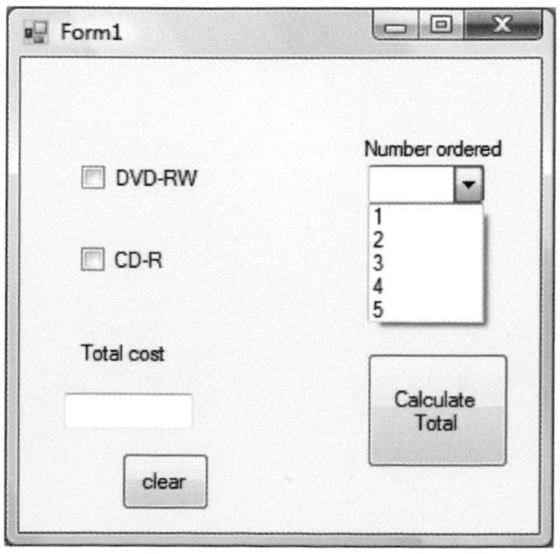

This example uses a combobox to input the number of the customer's order. Use a combobox + label, two checkboxes, a textbox + label and a button to calculate the total cost depending on the user's selection.

Filling the combobox

When you have inserted your combobox, you need to fill it with the numbers 1, 2, 3, 4, 5, which will be shown to the user. Follow these steps:

- Click on the combobox.
- Select the item's property.
- Click on the collection tab.

A window will open up in which you enter the numbers you want to display, one number on each line as shown in the screenshot below.

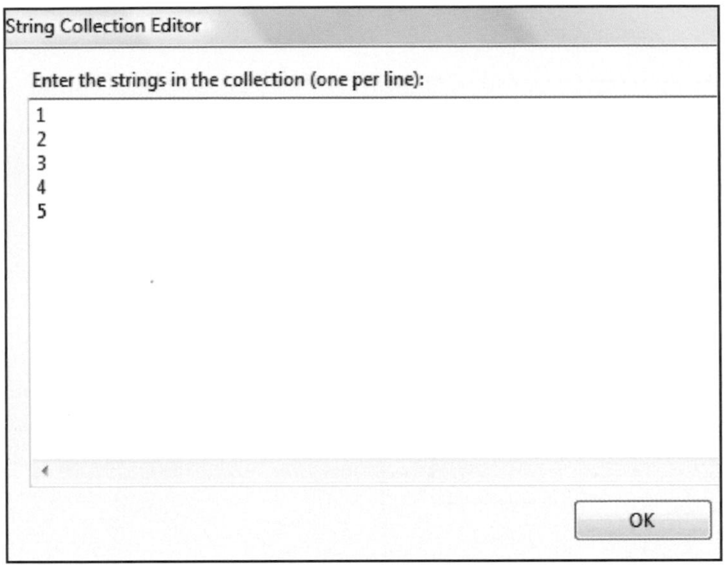

The coding is given below:

```
Dim ordernumber As Integer
Dim DVDRWcost As Single
Dim CDRcost As Single
Dim total_dvd_cost As Single
Dim total_CDR_cost As Single
Dim Overall_cost As Single
ordernumber = ComboBox1.Text
DVDRWcost = 50
CDRcost = 25
If CheckBox1.Checked = True Then
    total_dvd_cost = (DVDRWcost * ordernumber)
End If
If CheckBox2.Checked = True Then
    total_CDR_cost = (CDRcost * ordernumber)
End If
Overall_cost = total_dvd_cost + total_CDR_cost
    Totalbox.Text = Overall_cost
```

Note: You can use *if…elseif…end if* to get the same result.

Save your program as *Comboexample*.

Activities

29 Write a program using a combobox to enter and display the user's choice of song to download.
   You must produce the pseudocode for this program.
   Save it as Visual Basic Activity 29.

30 Write a program to calculate the cost of the air tickets for a family of up to five in number. The cost of tickets is as follows:

Economy seat	£100
Premium seat	£180

The program should enable the user to clear the display of the cost and enter new choices.
You must produce the pseudocode for this program.
Save it as Visual Basic Activity 30.

Using pre-defined functions

Functions are code that carries out an operation and then returns a result to your program.

Here are some functions that work with numbers.

The INT and ROUND functions

The INT function takes in a number and gives back the whole number or INTeger part of it. It ignores anything after the decimal point:

- number– INT(3.54) would produce 3
- number= INT(3.14) would produce 3

The ROUND function will round the numeric value to the nearest whole number:

- number= ROUND(3.54) would produce 4
- number= ROUND(3.14) would produce 3

Random

This generates a random number.

If you want a random whole number between 0 and 10 then use:

```
DIM RandomNumber as integer
RandomNumber = Rnd() * 10
MsgBox(RandomNumber)
```

For a random number between 0 and 50 change the middle line to:

```
RandomNumber = Rnd() * 50
```

and so on.

Activities

31 Write a program to fill an array with five random numbers between 1 and 100 and display the results in a listbox. Run your program and then stop. Run it again. What do you notice about the numbers? Save it as Visual Basic Activity 31.

32 Write a program that will produce a different series of random numbers each time a button is pressed. Save it as Visual Basic Activity 32.

Note: If you want to repeatedly enter random numbers in your program you have to use the command *Randomise()*.

If you don't use it then the same pattern of numbers will appear again and again.

So your coding would look like this:

```
DIM RandomNumber as integer
Randomise()
     RandomNumber = Rnd() * 10
     MsgBox(RandomNumber)
```

These functions work with strings:

Name	What it does	Example
Len	Calculates the number of characters in a string	Len("Blob") returns 4
UCase	Converts lowercase characters into uppercase characters	UCase("blob") returns BLOB
LCase	Converts uppercase characters into lowercase characters	LCase("Hello There") returns hello there
Asc	Returns the ASCII value of a character	Asc("A") returns 65
Chr	Takes an ASCII value and returns the corresponding character	Chr(65) returns A
Mid	Extracts a sub-string from a string	Mid("Word",2,3) returns "ord"

Activities

33 Try out some examples using your own first name as the string.
   - There is some code below to help you.
   - Use five buttons to try out the string functions.
   - Decide which button each piece of code has to be attached to. ⇨

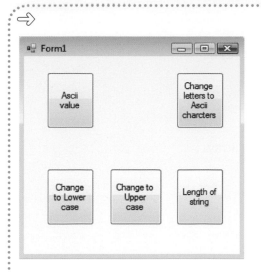

```
Dim Myname As String
Myname = "Fred"
MsgBox("Your name has " & Len(Myname) & " letters")
Dim Myname As String
Myname = "Fred"
MsgBox("Your name has changed from Fred to " & UCase(Myname))
Dim Myname As String
Myname = "Fred"
MsgBox("Your name has changed from Fred to " & LCase(Myname))
MsgBox("The ascii value of letter F is " & Asc("F"))
MsgBox("Number 69 in the Ascii code is letter " & Chr(69))
```

Save it as Visual Basic Activity 33.

Now try this coding out to help you find someone's initials:

```
Dim firstname, secondname As String
Dim initial1, initial2 As String
firstname = InputBox("Enter first name please")
secondname = InputBox("Enter second name please")
initial1 = Mid$(firstname, 1, 1)
initial2 = Mid$(secondname, 1, 1)
MsgBox("Your initials are " & initial1 & " " & initial2)
```

Activities

34 Write a program to make and display a user name for someone which combines the first three letters of each of their first name and their second name.

The program will then test the user name has been entered correctly before allowing the user to order CDs and display the total cost.

Save it as Visual Basic Activity 34.

Using arrays

An array is a list of numbers or words. Each array has a name. This array is called *Name*.

Index	0	1	2	3
Name	Fred	Ted	Ed	Ned

Each array has an index. The index is used to count down (or up) the array.

Note: visual basic starts counting from 0.

So *Name(0)* is Fred, *Name(1)* is Ted and so on.

This array is called *Prices*.

Index	0	1	2	3
Prices	34.99	12.50	14.30	56.00

Here *Prices(0)* is 34.99, *Prices(1)* is 12.50 and so on.

Setting up and filling an array

The first thing you have to do is set up your array using the DIM instruction, for example DIM Name(4) as string.

               size   type

This sets up an array called *Name* with five spaces that can hold text.

Next you have to use a loop to fill the array:

```
For index = 0 To 4
      Name(index) = InputBox("Enter a name")
Next index
```

Don't forget to set up your index:

```
DIM index As Integer
```

Time to get started!
- Open a new project.
- Add a button to start filling the array.
- Add a listbox to display the names in your array. Call it *Nameslist*.
- Add a label above your listbox. The text of the label should read 'Names'.

Your form should look like the screenshot below:

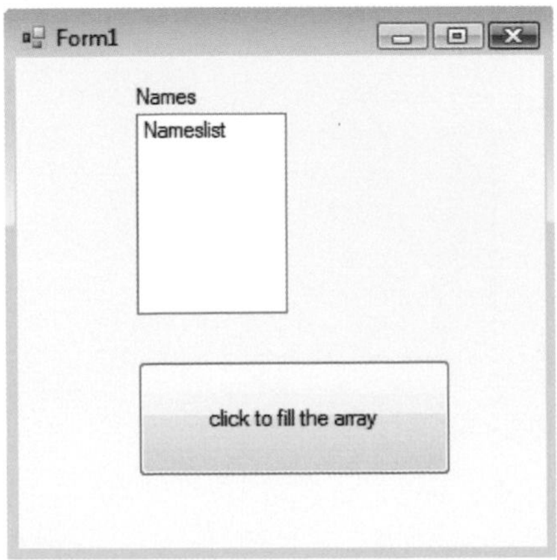

Remember

Before you add your code: Visual Basic starts numbering from 0.

Pseudocode

1. Initialise

2. Loop to fill array

3. Loop to display array contents

1.1 Set up array called *name* with five spaces

1.2 Set up index as an integer

2.1 Loop five times

2.2 Input name into array using index

3.1 Loop five times

3.2 Display names in array using index

Now add the following code to your button:

```
Dim Name(4) As String ' This sets up the array called name with five spaces
Dim index As Integer
For index = 0 To 4 ' This loop fills the array
    Name(index) = InputBox("Enter a name")
Next index
For index = 0 To 4 ' This loop displays the array in a listbox
    Nameslist.Items.Add(Name(index))
Next index
```

Don't forget to call your listbox *Nameslist*.

Test your program by entering five names.

Your form should look something like the screenshot below:

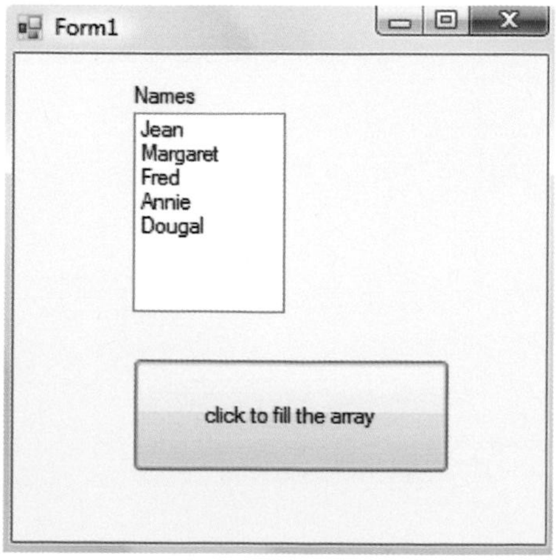

Save your program as *Array1*.

Note: Using one loop to fill the array and another loop to display the names means that the names don't appear in the listbox until you have entered all the names.

Change your program so that the names appear as you type them in. Change the coding to read:

```
Dim name(4) As String
Dim index As Integer
For index = 0 To 4 ' This loop fills the array
    name(index) = InputBox("Enter a name ")
    Nameslist.Items.Add(name(index)) ' This line puts the array contents
    into a listbox
Next index
```

This version only uses one loop and so is more efficient.

Test your program and save it as *Array2*.

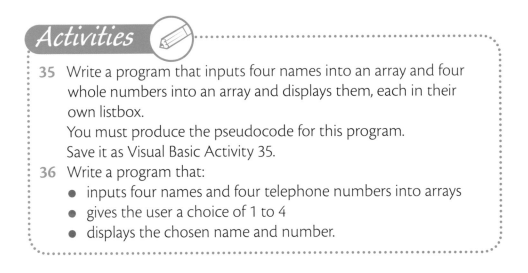

Activities

35 Write a program that inputs four names into an array and four whole numbers into an array and displays them, each in their own listbox.
You must produce the pseudocode for this program.
Save it as Visual Basic Activity 35.

36 Write a program that:
- inputs four names and four telephone numbers into arrays
- gives the user a choice of 1 to 4
- displays the chosen name and number.

Using the random function

The random function generates a random number.

If you want a random whole number between 0 and 10 then use:

```
DIM RandomNumber As Integer
Randomise()
RandomNumber = Rnd() * 10
MsgBox(RandomNumber)
```

For a random number between 0 and 50 change the third line to:

```
RandomNumber = Rnd() * 50
```

and so on.

Activities

37 Write a program to fill an array with five random numbers between 1 and 100 and display the results in a listbox.
Run your program and then stop. Run it again. What do you notice about the numbers?
Save it as Visual Basic Activity 37.

Activities

Super Task 6

Write a program to:

- store the names and costs of five movie DVDs
- ask for the name of a movie DVD on the list and display the name and price
- display an error message if the movie requested by the user is not on the list!

You need to complete a report for Super Task 6. The report should contain:

- a description of the task
- your pseudocode
- a table with test data that you have produced.

You should ask your teacher to check:

- your report
- your coding
- your test run and test data table.

You have now finished your National 5 Visual basic Programming.

Next step: on to Higher Programming!

Chapter 3

Reading and Interpreting Code

Design notation

In the design phase the problem is broken down into 'chunks' and each 'chunk' is then broken down further and further until the little bits are easy to solve in any programming language. The solution to the problem is called the *algorithm*, a fancy word for a plan. The process of repeatedly breaking the problem into smaller and smaller steps is called *stepwise refinement*, but you are not expected to remember the term in the exam. You might choose to use a graphical design notation or pseudocode to help you to solve the problem.

Graphical design notation

Examples of graphical design notations are structure diagrams, flow charts or simple block diagrams. Structure diagrams use boxes to show how the various subtasks in the problem break down into a tree-like structure. Flow charts use different-shaped boxes to show the kind of command or instruction to be used as shown in the diagram on the right. Diamonds are used for choices (like *If*), rounded rectangles are used for loops and plain boxes are used for assignments and calculations. They are very

(N4) useful in showing flow of control. Simple block diagrams are used to show how the problem can be broken down.

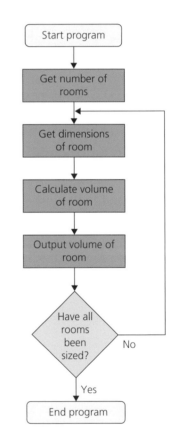

Problem

Write a program that will calculate the volume of a number of rooms. The program will first ask how many rooms there are. The program will then ask for the dimensions of each room, calculate the volume and output the volume of each room in turn.

Disadvantages

The details of each of the stages are not given in the flow diagram, they will have to be described elsewhere. If this is also done graphically there will be quite a few diagrams to make sense of.

Advantages

The structure of the program is very clear. The flow of control in the program, the order of execution of blocks of code, is also clear.

Unified Modelling Language (UML)

Unified Modelling Language (UML) is a modelling language used in the development of object-oriented software. Two examples of UML are activity diagrams and use case diagrams.

Activity diagrams

Activity diagrams are constructed from a limited number of shapes, connected by arrows. Below are some of the most important shape types and what they represent:

- Rounded rectangles represent activities
- Diamonds represent decisions
- Bars represent the start (split) or end (join) of concurrent activities
- A black circle represents the end (final state).

The artwork below shows an activity diagram for a piece of online shopping software.

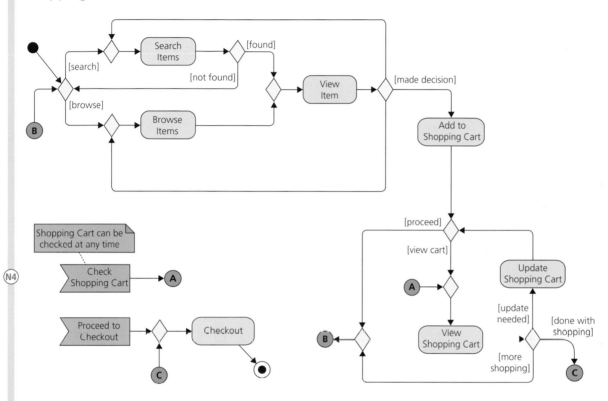

Use case diagrams

Use case diagrams are used to represent how a programme or system functions. It gives a straightforward, top level, at-a-glance description of how it works. An example of a use case diagram from a customer order system is shown below.

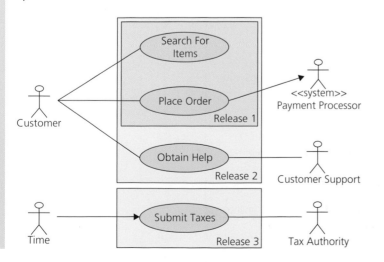

Pseudocode

Pseudocode is a code-like description of the stages involved in solving a task. It is closer to English than a programming language and it helps us to write out and understand how to solve the problem. Below is a simple example of the use of pseudocode.

Example 🚩

Problem

Write a program that will calculate the volume of a number of rooms. The program will first ask how many rooms there are. The program will then ask for the dimensions of each room, calculate the volume and output the volume of each room in turn.

Algorithm in pseudocode

Main program

1 Ask user for the number of rooms, store in number
2 Start of fixed loop (1 to number)
3 Ask for dimensions of room
4 Calculate volume as length × breadth × height
5 Display volume of room
6 End of fixed loop
7 End program

Refinement of step 3

3.1 Ask for length of room, store in length
3.2 Ask for breadth of room, store in breadth
3.3 Ask for height of room, store in height

Key points ❗

Readability

Programmers should make sure that their program is readable, so that other people can understand the code and maintain it if necessary. They can do this by using:

* **Meaningful identifiers (names)**
  The names of all variables, arrays and sub-routines should give some indication of what they hold or do, for example: Surname$, TaxRate, PassMark, SquirrelCounter, ComputingMarks( )

* **Internal commentary**
  Internal documentation, or comments/remarks, can give information about what a piece of code does, for example: total = total + mark ' *this adds up the marks using a running total*

* **Indentation**
  Indentation of the lines of code within loops or *If* statements can make the structure of the code more obvious.

Below is an example of code that is not readable and an example of code that is!

Poor code	Readable code

let x = 0
print "pass mark";
input a
for p = 1 to 20
print "mark";
input m
if m>=p then let x =x+1
next p
print x;"passed"
end
	!A program to count the number of passes
	!in a class of 20. All marks are percentages.
	LET count = 0
	PRINT "What is the pass mark";
	INPUT pass
	FOR pupil = 1 TO 20
	    PRINT "What is the mark for pupil"; pupil; "?"
	    INPUT mark
	    IF mark >= pass THEN
	    LET count = count + 1
	    END IF
	NEXT pupil
	PRINT "A total of"; count; "pupils passed the test."
	END

Variables

Any program that you write will have to store values while it works. For this we use variables. Think of these as labelled boxes containing values you will need to store for later use.

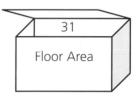

Type of variable	Examples	Level
String variables: hold text	Fred, Jean, Doughnut	4
Integers variables: hold positive or negative whole numbers	12, 45, 100, −32, −42	4
Real variables: hold floating point numbers	78.2346, 44.872	5
Boolean variables: hold true/false values	Dim Correct As Boolean = False	5

(N4)

Key points ❗

Input and output

A common way of getting values into variables is to ask the user to input them at the keyboard. Each software development environment has its own way of outputting the variable. Scratch does it by displaying a graphic and/or by having a sprite 'say' the variable value as shown in the screenshot in the table.

Scratch	Visual Basic
CD Name Amaright Ameringue Amaright Ameringue	'Simple input/output demo Teamname = InputBox("enter team's name") Teamname.Text = Teamname
	cd_cost = InputBox("Enter the cost of a CD in pence please") MsgBox("The cost in pence = " & cd_cost)

Assigning variables

Another way of putting a value into a variable is to set it in the coding as shown in the screenshot in the table.

Scratch	Visual Basic
!Assignment example set CD Name ▾ to 7.99	'Assignment examples Dim score As Integer = 0 Dim Question As String = "What is the Capital of Sweden?" Dim answer As String = "Stockholm"

Arithmetic operators

These tend to be common across all programming languages.

adding	+
subtraction	−
multiplying	*
division	/
Power of	^

Key points !

Fixed loops

When you have a piece of code that you want the computer to repeat a set number of times, you would use a fixed loop as shown in the screenshot in the table:

Scratch	Visual Basic
when ⚑ clicked repeat 5 ask Enter the name of a pupil in your class and wait set Name of pupil ▾ to answer	'Fixed Loop example For counter = 1 to 5 name = Inputbox("Enter the name of a pupil in your class please") Msgbox("The name you entered was " & name) Next

Conditional statements (*If*)

A conditional statement is a way of making a choice in a programming language. A simple *If* statement allows you to choose to do or not to do an action. Groups of actions can be contained in *if* statements and, by using *if…then…else*, you can choose one 'branch' over another. The code in the following table gives examples of each of these uses of *if*.

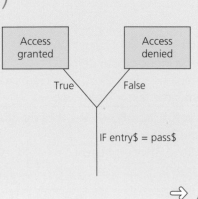

⇨

Scratch	Visual Basic

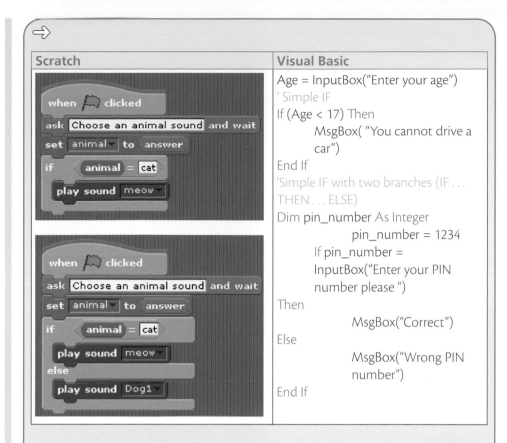	Age = InputBox("Enter your age")
	' Simple IF
	If (Age < 17) Then
	      MsgBox("You cannot drive a
	      car")
	End If
	'Simple IF with two branches (IF . . .
	THEN . . . ELSE)
	Dim pin_number As Integer
	      pin_number = 1234
	      If pin_number =
	      InputBox("Enter your PIN
	      number please ")
	Then
	      MsgBox("Correct")
	Else
	      MsgBox("Wrong PIN
	      number")
	End If

(N4) Conditional loops

It may be that you want to do something more than once, but you don't know how often you will need to do it. Here is where the conditional loop comes in.

This will allow you to set a condition to allow the program to leave the loop.

Scratch	Visual Basic

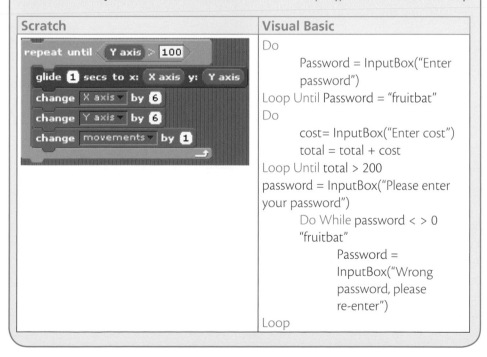	Do
	      Password = InputBox("Enter
	      password")
	Loop Until Password = "fruitbat"
	Do
	      cost= InputBox("Enter cost")
	      total = total + cost
	Loop Until total > 200
	password = InputBox("Please enter
	your password")
	      Do While password < > 0
	      "fruitbat"
	      Password =
	      InputBox("Wrong
	      password, please
	      re-enter")
	Loop

Questions ?

1 Describe one advantage of using a graphical notation.
2 Describe one advantage of using pseudocode.
3 Read the following code and then answer the questions that follow.

```
Dim counter As Integer
Dim number_of_tickets As Integer
Dim Day As String
Dim price As Single
Dim time As String
number_of_tickets = InputBox("Number of tickets please")
Day = InputBox("Which day?")
price = 500
time = InputBox("Time")
For counter = 1 To number_of_tickets names.Items.Add("Ticket number "
& counter & "on " & Day & "at " & time & "price £ " & price)
Next
```

   a) Describe the purpose of this line:
       Dim counter As Integer
   b) Explain the purpose of the counter.
   c) Describe the difference between these two ways of storing data in variables:
       ● number_of_tickets = InputBox("Number of tickets please")
       ● price = 500
   d) What could be done to improve the readability of the *for . . . next* loop?

4 Copy and complete this table matching the type to the variable.

Variable	Type
Smartphone	String
28	
130	
Alexander	
4.23	
114.83	

5 If you wanted to check whether a PIN number entry was correct, what kind of variable would you use?
6 Complete this sentence: 'One way to input data is to ask the user to input it at the keyboard. Another way is to _____ data to variables in the programs code.'
7 If you wanted to input five pupils' names and marks, what construct would you use?

8 Explain why the program in the screenshot below will not draw a proper hexagon.

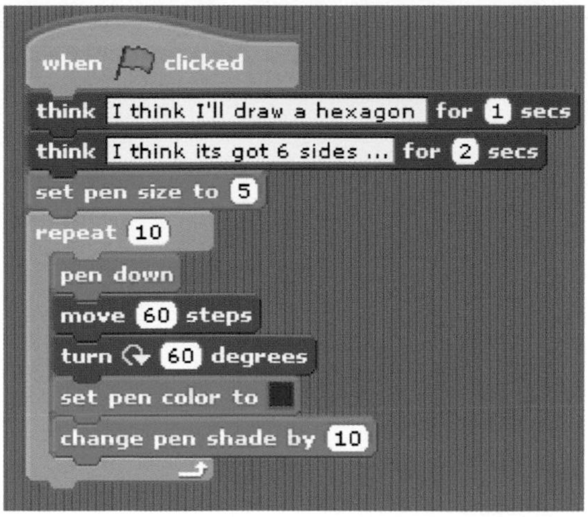

9 Read the following code carefully. Then answer the questions that follow.

```
Dim PIN_number As Integer
PIN_number = 1234
If PIN_number = InputBox("Enter your PIN number please") Then
     MsgBox("Correct")
End If
MsgBox("Wrong PIN number")
```

a) Why will this code always produce a wrong output?
b) How would you change the coding to produce the correct output?
c) What comment lines would you add to explain the purpose of line 1 and line 3?

10 Read the following code carefully. Then complete the tasks that follow.

```
password = InputBox("Please enter your password")
Do While password < > 0 "fruitbat"
password = InputBox("Wrong password, please re-enter")
Loop
```

a) Rewrite this code with suitable comment lines explaining lines 2 and 3.
b) Explain why a *repeat . . . until* loop would not be suitable here.

11 What should be added to the Scratch block in the screenshot below to make it correctly check a password entry?

⇨

12 Look carefully at the Scratch program in the screenshot below, then complete the table that follows. You can enter the coding and run it to help you understand what each instruction is doing.

say 'you can play an animal sound or a hiphop sound'	
ask 'choose a sound please' and wait	
if answer = animal	
play sound meow	
if answer = hiphop	
play sound HipHop	

(N4) 13 Look carefully at the Scratch program in the screenshot below, then complete the table that follows. You can enter the coding and run it to help you understand what each instruction is doing.

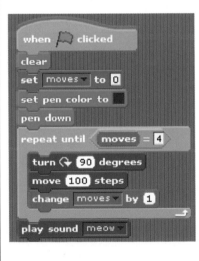

set moves to 0	
set pen colour to red	
repeat until moves = 4	
turn 90 degrees	
change moves by 1	
move 100 steps	
play sound 'meow'	

What you should know 👍

Complex conditions and the logical operators

The *If* statements and conditional loops contained simple conditions that were based on one thing being true or false. Complex conditions can depend on two or more things.

These conditions can be combined using the logical operators *AND*, *OR* and *NOT*.

★ For the whole *AND* condition to be *true*, *both* parts have to be *true*.

★ For the whole *OR* condition to be *true*, *either* part can be *true*.

★ For the *NOT* to be *true*, the condition it applies to must be *false*.

To give an example of the difference between each of these, see the diagrams below. The shaded area in diagram A represents those pupils in a class who are *female AND* have *blue* eyes (the blue-eyed females only). The shaded area in diagram O represents those pupils in the class who are *female OR* have *blue* eyes (every female plus the blue-eyed boys). Diagram N shows those pupils who have *blue* eyes *AND* who are *NOT female*.

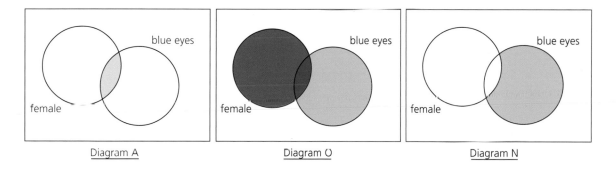

| Diagram A | Diagram O | Diagram N |

The following examples of code illustrate the use of AND, OR and NOT.

Scratch	Visual Basic

if `mark < 0 or mark > 100`
 say `that mark is out of range`
 	
 repeat until `points > 200 and fuel < 300`
 change `top score` by `20`
 	
 if `not password = Meringue`
 say `wrong password`
	Age = InputBox("Enter your age")
	 If (Age >= 17 AND Age <= 70) Then
	     MsgBox("You can donate blood.")
	 End If
	 If (Age < 17 OR Age > 70) Then
	     MsgBox("You cannot donate blood.")
	 End If
	 If Not(Age >= 17) Then
	     MsgBox("You are too young to donate.")
	 End If

Key points !

Pre-defined functions

A pre-defined function is a section of code that has been written, checked, tested, translated and saved in a function library for later use by other programmers. There are many useful pre-defined functions in any programming language. A few from Visual Basic are given below (however, there may be slight grammar differences in other languages).

* RND gives a random real number between 0 and 1.
* RANDOMIZE gives a new random number each time RND is used.
* INT(grade) takes the value in the variable, here called grade, and drops the numbers after the decimal point, i.e. INT(3.87) has the value 3.
* ROUND(num) rounds a number to the nearest whole number.
* ROUND(num,2) rounds the number to two decimal places.

These functions work with string variables.

Name	What it does	Example
Len	Calculates the number of characters in a string	Len("Blob") returns 4
UCase	Converts lowercase characters into uppercase characters	UCase("blob") returns BLOB
LCase	Converts uppercase characters into lowercase characters	LCase("Hello There") returns hello there
Asc	Returns the ASCII value of a character	Asc("A") returns 65
Chr	Takes an ASCII value and returns the corresponding character	Chr(65) returns A
Mid	Extracts a sub-string from a string	Mid("Word",2,3) returns "ord"

In Scratch there is a range of functions to choose from:

`join hello world`	joins two strings
`length of world`	gives the length of a string
`letter 1 of world`	gives a specific letter in a string
`round ◯`	round to the nearest whole number
`◯ mod ◯`	gives the remainder after an arithmetic operation
`pick random 1 to 10`	gives a random number in a specified range
abs sqrt sin cos tan asin acos atan ln log e ^ 10 ^	gives a range of mathematical functions

Functions return a value to a program. The value is returned using a 'parameter'. A parameter is a variable which holds value being passed from the function to the main program.

What you should know 👍

Using arrays

An array is a list of numbers or words. Each array has a name. This array is called *Name*.

INDEX	1	2	3	4
Name	Fred	Ted	Ed	Ned

Each array has an index. The index is used to count down (or up) the array.

So *Name(1)* is Fred, *Name(2)* is Ted and so on.

This array is called *Prices*.

Index	1	2	3	4
Prices	34.99	12.50	14.30	56.00

Here *Prices(1)* is 34.99, *Prices(2)* is 12.50 and so on.

Scratch	Visual Basic

when 🏳 clicked
repeat 5
  ask Enter the name of the grocery item and wait
  insert answer at 1▾ of Grocery Items▾
	'Code for filling an array
	Dim name(4) As String
	Dim mark(4) As Integer
	    Dim index As Integer
	    For index = 0 To 4
	        name(index) =
	        InputBox("Enter a
	        name")
	        mark(index) =
	        InputBox("Enter a
	        mark")
	    Next index

Key points ❗

Testing phase

Once the code has been entered, and all the typing mistakes removed, it has to be tested with a range of inputs to make sure that it does the job it is meant to do and that it does not keep crashing all the time. The three areas of input that have to be tested are *normal*, *extreme* and *exceptional*. These are also called 'in range', 'boundary' and 'out of range'. Below is a table of test data to fully test a sub-routine validating data input as whole percentages.

Normal (in range)	Extreme (boundary)	Exceptional (out of range)
6, 21, 57, 99 (4 items between 0 and 100)	0, 100 (extremes of the range)	−1, 101, 69.2 (below, above, non-integer)

Syntax

This is an error resulting from breaking the rules of the language, for example:

```
If total > 100 Then
Print "You have exceeded the maximum"
End
```

The missing *if* will produce an error message.

Execution error

This is an error that prevents a program from running, for example calling a sub-routine that has not been written or a variable that has not been declared. See screenshot below.

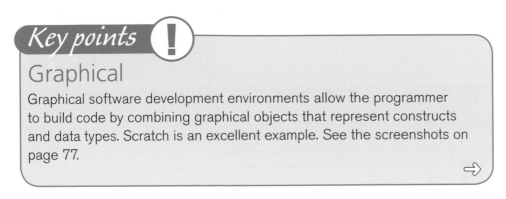

Logic error

This is an error that produces incorrect results but does not stop the program from running. It is caused by an error in the design of the program, such as a badly written complex condition:

```
If total < 1 Or total > 99 Then... fails to correctly check a range of
between 0 and 100
```

Graphical and text-based software development environments

Key points !

Graphical

Graphical software development environments allow the programmer to build code by combining graphical objects that represent constructs and data types. Scratch is an excellent example. See the screenshots on page 77.

⇨

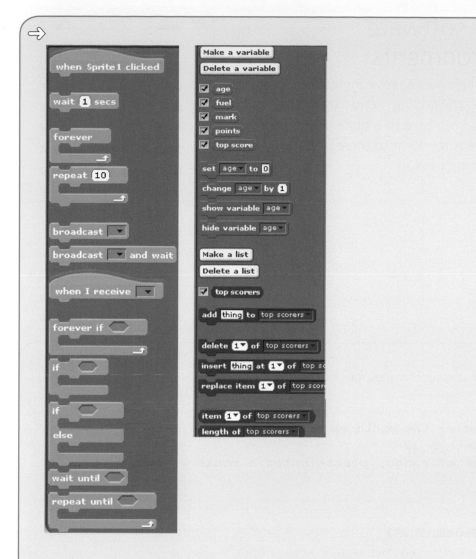

Text-based

Examples of text-based software development environments are Truebasic, Pascal and Visual Basic. When you use one of these you have to type in the programming code instructions.

Here is an example from Visual Basic:

```
For counter = 1 To 5
    mark = InputBox("Enter a mark between 0 and
    100.")
    Do While mark < 0 Or mark > 100
        mark = InputBox("Out of range. Please
        enter a mark between 0 and 100.")
    Loop
    total = total + mark
    Total_marks.Text = total
Next
average = total / 5
Average_mark.Text = average
```

Editing features of software development environments

The editing features vary from environment to environment. For example, the screenshot to the right shows the editing menu from Visual Basic.

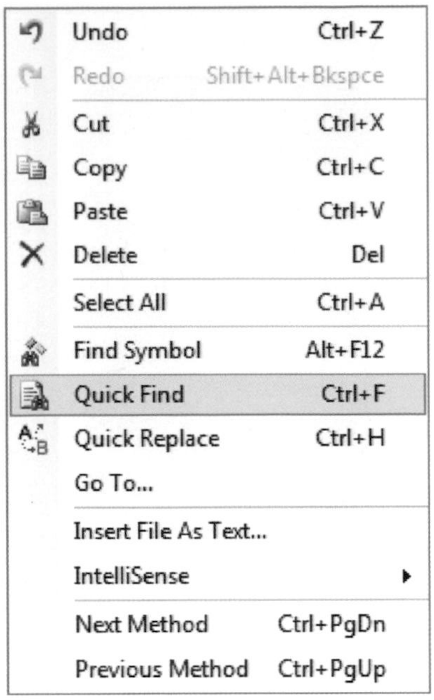

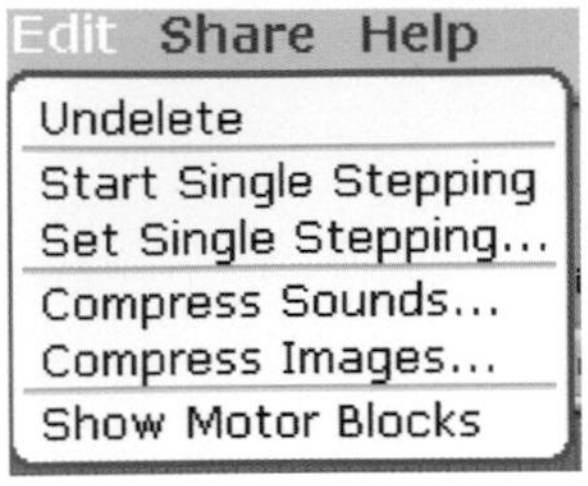

Undo Ctrl+Z
Redo Shift+Alt+Bkspce
Cut Ctrl+X
Copy Ctrl+C
Paste Ctrl+V
Delete Del
Select All Ctrl+A
Find Symbol Alt+F12
Quick Find Ctrl+F
Quick Replace Ctrl+H
Go To...
Insert File As Text...
IntelliSense
Next Method Ctrl+PgDn
Previous Method Ctrl+PgUp

In comparison, the editing menu from Scratch is quite limited, but then Scratch is not a text-based environment so there is less need for text-based editing. See the screenshot below.

Edit Share Help
Undelete
Start Single Stepping
Set Single Stepping...
Compress Sounds...
Compress Images...
Show Motor Blocks

Questions ?

14 Read the following code, then answer the questions that follow.

```
Dim XX As Integer
XX = InputBox("Please enter the month as a number.")
Do While XX < 0 Or month > 12
     XX = InputBox("Out of range, please enter a month > than 0 < 13.")
Loop
Select Case month
Case Is = 12
MsgBox("You entered December.")
Case Is = 11
MsgBox("You entered November.")
End Select
```

a) Suggest a suitable variable name for the user's input.

b) Write a comment line to explain the purpose of the third line.

c) Describe how the use of indentation would make it easier to follow the operation of:

(i) the *Do . . . while* loop

(ii) the Case construct.

15 Examine the Scratch program in the screenshot below and then answer the questions that follow.

when clicked
go to x: -190 y: -126
set x axis to 0
set Y axis to 0
set movements to 0
repeat until movements = 24 or Y axis = 120
glide 1 secs to x: x axis y: Y axis
change x axis by 5
change Y axis by 5
change movements by 1

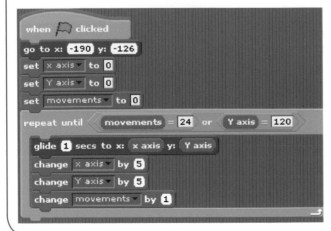

⇨
a) Explain the purpose of the complex condition.
b) Describe the effect of the lines changing the X and Y axis values inside
the loop.

16 Look carefully at the Scratch program in the screenshot below, then
complete the table that follows. You can enter the coding and run it to
help you understand what each instruction is doing.

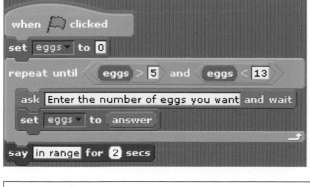

set size to answer	
if size > 20	
ask 'that's too big make it less than 21'	
set size to answer	
set pen size to size	
pen down	
set pen colour to 30	
repeat 8	
move 40 steps	
turn 45 degrees	

17 Look carefully at the Scratch program in the screenshot below, then
complete the table that follows. You can enter the coding and run it to
help you understand what each instruction is doing.

set eggs to 0	
repeat until eggs >5 and eggs <13	
ask ' enter the number of eggs you want and wait'	
set eggs to answer	
say ' in range for 2 seconds'	

18 Describe the purpose of the following functions: RND; RANDOMIZE;
INT; ROUND; LEN; CHR; MOD.

⇨

19 Read the coding below and then complete the text that follows.

```
Dim price As Integer
price = Read_number.Text
If price > 50 Then
    MsgBox("The price you entered was greater than 50")
End If
```

In line 1, the variable number is set up to store a _____ number.
In line 2, the user enters the number to be stored in the _____ price
using a _____. In line 3, the *If* _____ to see if the number stored in
the variable price is _____ than 50. In line 4, a message is _____ if the
price is greater than 50.
Wordbank: variable, textbox, greater, displayed, checks, whole

20 Read the coding below and then answer the questions that follow.

```
Dim names As String
Dim counter As Integer
For counter = 1 To 5
names = InputBox("Please enter a name")
MsgBox("You entered " & names)
Next
```

a) Explain what is happening in line 1.
b) Explain what is happening in line 2.
c) What is the counter used for in line 3?
d) Describe what happens in line 4.

21 Read the code below carefully and answer the questions that follow.

```
Dim mark As Integer
Dim counter As Integer
Dim total As Integer
Dim average As Single 'this can store…
For counter = 1 To 5
mark = InputBox("Enter a mark between 0 and 100.")
Do While mark < 0 Or mark > 100
    mark = InputBox("Out of range. Please enter a mark between 0 and
    100.")
Loop
total = total + mark
Total_marks.Text = total
Next
        average = total / 5
        Average_mark.Text = average
```

a) Complete the comment line on line 4.
b) Explain what the 'While' loop is doing in line 7.
c) How is the total being calculated and displayed?

⇨

22 Read the code below carefully and answer the questions that follow.

```
Dim firstname, secondname As String
    Dim initial1, initial2 As String
    firstname = InputBox("Enter first name please")
    secondname = InputBox("Enter second name please")
    initial1 = Mid$(firstname, 1, 1)
    initial2 = Mid$(secondname, 1, 1)
    MsgBox("Your initials are " & initial1 & " " & initial2")
```

a) What kind of variables are being initialised in line 2?
b) What will the variables being initialised in line 2 be used for?
c) What is being stored in the variable *initial1* in line 5?
d) What is the output in line 7?

23 Read the code carefully and answer the questions that follow.

```
Dim name(4) As String
Dim mark(4) As Integer
Dim index As Integer
For index = 0 To 4
    name(index) = InputBox("Enter a name")
    mark(index) = InputBox("Enter a mark")
Next index
For index = 0 To 4
    nameslist.Items.Add(name(index))
    markslist.Items.Add(mark(index))
Next index
```

a) What is being initialised in line 1?
b) What is being initialised in line 2?
c) What is the index being used for in **(i)** line 4? **(ii)** line 5?
d) Explain what the instruction in line 9 does.

24 Read the code below carefully and answer the questions that follow.

```
Dim waistsize As Integer
waistsize = readingwaist.Text
Select Case waistsize ' checks waist sizes and gives sizes of jeans
    Case Is >= 60
        outputjeansize.Text = "XX Large"
    Case Is >= 50 And waistsize < 60
        outputjeansize.Text = "X Large"
    Case Is > 40 And waistsize < 50
        outputjeansize.Text = "Large"
    Case Is > 30 And waistsize < 40
        outputjeansize.Text = "Medium"
    Case Is > 20 And waistsize <30
        outputjeansize.Text = "Small"
End Select
```

a) Explain what the instruction in line 4 is doing.
b) Describe the operation of the complex condition in line 10.
c) Describe what the instruction in line 11 does.

Comparing two contemporary software development environments

To complete your National 5 unit you have to compare two contemporary software development environments (programming languages). You need to:

- compare the range of data types provided by each one
- describe how each represents standard constructs
- compare their editing features
- describe how high-level code is translated and executed.

Now you have read all about 'Reading and Interpreting Code' and answered all the questions, you should be in a good position to make the comparison between Scratch and Visual Basic. Even if you are using another two programming languages this should have given you plenty of ideas about how to approach this task.

Here are some example standard constructs to help you:

Scratch	Visual Basic
Data types	
Allows you to store both string and numeric variables but you don't have to declare them as being different. It does not have Boolean variables.	Has a complete range of variables: integer, real, string and Boolean.
Has arrays that can hold either strings or numbers.	Allows you to declare arrays of any size to hold any type of data.
Constructs	
If	If
If else	If then else
fixed loop	fixed loop
loop with condition at start of loop	loop with condition at start of loop loop with condition at end of loop
loop continuously	
'wait' using a timer	
arithmetic operators	arithmetic operators
comparison operators	comparison operators
logical operators	logical operators
predefined functions	a wider range of predefined functions, particularly when manipulating string variables
Editing	
Has limited editing features since it is based on manipulating graphical objects that represent the constructs and data types, for example. Ease of manipulation of instructions is its strong point rather than control over editing.	Has a wide range to editing features that enable you to copy and paste, cut, find and replace, for example, altogether giving you much more control over the editing process.
Prevents syntax errors since the instructions blocks are already built. It can't prevent logic errors though!	It has an error feedback that can help detect and correct errors.
Translation	
Scratch is written in a language called Squeak, which is compiled.	Compiled

Chapter 4

Low Level Operation and Structure

Computer systems

★ have at their core a processor which acts as the 'brains' of the computer

★ store data in memory

★ use buses to move data around, for example, to transfer data to and from the memory

★ use interfaces to communicate with external devices such as printers, monitors, cameras, games controllers, etc.

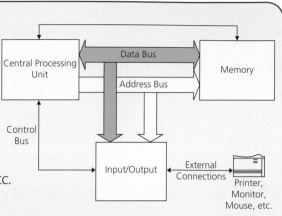

Concatenation

Concatenation is the adding together of strings. Below is an example from Visual Basic and Scratch which will display the word *doughnut* on the computer screen. The ampersand (&) is a common operator for concatenation in text-based languages like Visual Basic.

Scratch	Visual Basic
when 🏳 clicked set firstword to dough set second word to nut set thirdword to join firstword second word think thirdword	Dim firstword, secondword, thirdword As String firstword = "dough" secondword = "nut" thirdword = firstword & secondword MsgBox(thirdword)

The processor

The processor is at the centre of all of the computer's operations and deals with all the movement of data and any calculations to be carried out. A processor is a number of layers of silicon crystal wafers on which millions of tiny electronic components are etched. It is made up of three important components: the Control Unit (CU), the Arithmetic and Logic Unit (ALU), and Registers.

Control Unit

This sends control signals which allow data to be stored in memory, fetched from memory, and which decode and carry out instructions.

Arithmetic and Logic Unit

This carries out all of the computer's arithmetic and logical functions. Arithmetic functions are functions such as addition, subtraction and multiplication. Logic functions are functions like comparing values using IF, AND, OR, >, <, and equals.

Registers

Registers are storage locations that are internal to the processor. They are used to:

- store data that is being transferred to or from memory
- hold the address of the location in memory which the processor is accessing to read or write data
- hold the instructions that are being carried out.

Computer memory

Main memory can be either RAM or ROM. RAM is the working space of the computer. It holds all of the programs and data files currently in use by the system and users. ROM is system memory which holds vital systems information, for example start-up instructions.

RAM: Random Access Memory

- The processor can write to, or read from, RAM at high speed.
- Data held in RAM *can* be changed.
- All data in RAM is *lost* when the power is switched off.
- RAM holds all the data and programs currently in use.

ROM: Read Only Memory

- Data is stored permanently in ROM – it is *not lost* when the power is switched off.
- Data in ROM *cannot* be changed.
- ROM holds vital systems data and programs.

Buses

Buses are used as transmitters between the different parts of a computer system. The two main buses are the data bus, and the address bus.

The data bus

The lines on the data bus provide a path for data to be transferred between system modules, for example, between main memory and the processor.

The number of lines of data = the width of the bus. Each line can carry one bit, therefore a 32-bit data bus can transfer 32 bits at a time. The width of the data bus is important when determining how efficiently a system performs.

The address bus

The address bus holds the address of the memory location where data is about to be stored or from which data is about to be read. In theory, the more lines on the address bus, the more locations the system can address.

The control bus

The control bus is not like the other two buses. It is a series of independent control lines used to send out control signals like 'read from memory' and 'write to memory'.

Interfaces

An interface is the combination of hardware and software needed to link the processor to the peripherals, and is the means by which independent systems can communicate, despite their differing characteristics. Computer peripherals such as CD-ROM drives, scanners, keyboards, etc., all have different characteristics, for example:

- They all have different transfer rates.
- They use a wide variety of codes and control signals.
- Some transmit data in serial form and others in parallel form.
- Some (for example, keyboards) work at higher voltages than the processor.
- They all operate at much slower speeds than the processor.

To remove these problems and allow the processor and peripherals to communicate, an interface will do jobs such as:

- change electrical voltages
- deal with control signals
- change analogue data into digital form
- store incoming data so that the processor can get on with other tasks.

Data representation

Using binary to represent positive numbers

We use the decimal numbers 0, 1, 2, 3, 4, 5, 6, 7, 8, 9.

Computers use binary numbers. To work with decimals, the computer has to convert them to binary. The table below will help you understand how to convert them.

2^7	2^6	2^5	2^4	2^3	2^2	2^1	2^0	Power of 2
128	64	32	16	8	4	2	1	Decimal equivalent

(N4) The decimal number 66 is stored as 01000010 in binary.

2^7	2^6	2^5	2^4	2^3	2^2	2^1	2^0	Power of 2
128	64	32	16	8	4	2	1	Decimal
0	1	0	0	0	0	1	0	= 64 + 2 = 66

Text

Text is represented using ASCII code. ASCII stands for **A**merican **S**tandard **C**ode for **I**nformation **I**nterchange.

ASCII is a 7-bit code which provides 128 code values: this gives us 96 characters and 32 control codes. Many systems use extended ASCII code, which is an 8-bit code that gives a range of 256 characters.

Each of the characters in the character set – all the characters available to the user – has a unique value. All characters are included:

- Non-printing characters such as <return>, <tab>, <escape>
- Upper and lower case letters such as A–Z, a–z
- Numbers such as 0–9
- Punctuation and other symbols such as $ & * ^ @ " :

An extract of the binary code is shown in the table:

Binary	Decimal	Representing
01000001	65	A
01000010	66	B
01000011	67	C
01000100	68	D
01000101	69	E
01000110	70	F

Unicode

Unicode is a 16-bit code which supports 65,536 characters. This is many more than ASCII code, and enables Unicode to define codes for

- every character-based alphabet in the world
- large, ideographic languages like Chinese, Japanese and Korean
- all punctuation symbols and control characters.

The first 256 values in Unicode are used to represent ASCII code, which makes conversion between the two codes easy. Of the 65,536 characters in Unicode, 49,000 codes are predefined and 6,400 are reserved for private use. This means that codes can be defined by the user or by software. This still leaves around 10,000 characters in the code that have not yet been made use of, which keeps them available for future developments.

What you should know 👍

Measuring the size of memory

We use these terms to measure the computer's memory.

Bit	Binary digit: a single 1 or 0
Byte	8 Bits, for example 11001110
Kilobyte	1024 Bytes
Megabyte	1024 Kilobytes
Gigabyte	1024 Megabytes
Terabyte	1024 Gigabytes

Machine code

Machine code is the language that the computer understands at the lowest level. In machine code, the instructions are made up of binary numbers and look like the box on the right.

The disadvantage is that they are very difficult to read and understand.

Programs written in high level languages like Visual Basic need to be translated into machine code.

```
01101101
11001100
01011100
11110000
```

Translators

Remember, at the lowest level, the system *only* understands machine code.

All programs written in a high level language need to be translated into machine code before the instructions can be carried out by the system. We use translator programs to carry out this translation. An example of this is shown below.

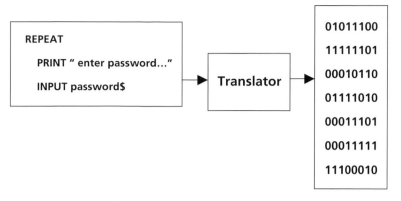

There are two different types of translator, each with its own advantages and disadvantages. They are compilers and interpreters.

Interpreter

An interpreter does not produce object code. The translator translates *and* executes *each* line of the program *in turn*.

Advantages of using an interpreter

- If errors are present, then they are highlighted immediately and are therefore easier to detect and fix.
- Interpreters can run partial code or code under development.

Disadvantages of using an interpreter

- As translation is *not* saved, the interpreter *must* be present to run code.
- If code is repeated, as in a loop, the code is translated and run *many* times.
- Individual runs are slower, due to the above two points.

Compiler

A compiler translates high level language instructions, called source code, into machine code, object code. It does this by going through the source one line at a time and translating it. It puts the translation in a file and moves on. When the whole program is translated the object code can be run. There is no need to translate the source again, unless the program is changed. If there are any syntax errors – errors in grammar – it lists them. The object code cannot be run until the whole program is translated.

Advantages of a compiler

- If no errors are found, then the source does not need to be translated again.
- The translator program is no longer required once the program is translated.

Disadvantages of a compiler

- If *any* syntax errors are present then the program will not run.
- The errors may be harder to correct, as problems may not be identified until the code is translated.

Representing black and white graphics, bit mapped graphics

Graphics (drawings, graphs or pictures) are made up of pixels, points on the screen. Look at the diagram on the right.

Each pixel is represented by patterns of binary numbers where each square or pixel filled in = 1, and each square or pixel left blank = 0.

For the representation of colour graphics, see page 109.

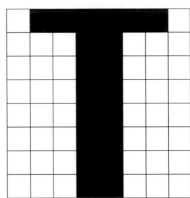

Vector graphics data

Vector graphics are another way of representing graphical data. A picture in a bit mapped graphic is made up of small squares of colour (pixels). In a vector, or object-oriented, graphic the image is made up of a number of shapes layered on top of one another to make up the picture.

Each object in the picture is described mathematically as a list of attributes. These fully describe the *type* of object, its *position* on screen, its *size* and the *colour/pattern* of its outline (called *line*) and middle (called *fill*). Other attributes might be the degree of any *rotation* and which *layer* it is on.

A typical object might be described in a vector graphics package as:
> line(layer, startX, startY, endX, endY, line colour, line thickness, line pattern)

These instructions, which describe the vector graphic, are then translated into bitmaps and binary numbers before the graphic can be displayed on the screen.

Representing real numbers

Real numbers are represented using floating point.

In floating point, numbers are divided into Base/Mantissa/Exponent.

Any number that is a power of 10 can be represented with a decimal point in a fixed position, so $13.75 = .13750 * 10^2$.

Decimal example – Binary example

Mantissa	Exponent	Base
.13750	2	10

Mantissa	Exponent	Base
1101110	100	2

Chapter 5

Researching and Reporting

What you have to do

To meet Outcome 3 of your National 4 unit you have to research and report on a contemporary software application by:

1 describing the software application.
This means you will need to describe the purpose of the application, its key features and also its interface.

2 thinking about how some of the programming constructs and variables that you have learned about are used in your chosen application.
You could, for example, think about how the application uses *integer* and *string variables*, or how it uses *if . . end if*, or how it uses *loops*.

3 considering the effect the application has on society or the environment.
You could think about how the application might help to reduce or increase use of resources, such as energy and paper. You might think about how the application might affect people's privacy, data security or online crime.

When you hand in your report you must include a page at the end where you state all the sources of your information.

Here is a sample report to guide you:

N4

Example 🏳

Firefox version 10

Firefox features

Firefox 10 is a freeware browser (see screenshot below). That means that you can install and use it for free. It is a powerful piece of software that helps you move around the Internet and look at web pages.

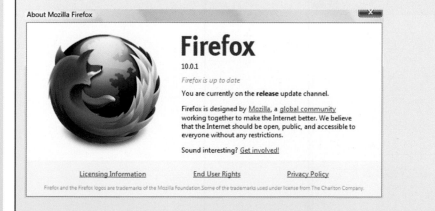

About Mozilla Firefox

Firefox

10.0.1

Firefox is up to date

You are currently on the **release** update channel.

Firefox is designed by Mozilla, a global community working together to make the Internet better. We believe that the Internet should be open, public, and accessible to everyone without any restrictions.

Sound interesting? Get involved!

Licensing Information   End User Rights   Privacy Policy

Firefox and the Firefox logos are trademarks of the Mozilla Foundation. Some of the trademarks used under license from The Charlton Company.

It is designed for fast performance and has safeguards against web pages crashing. It also has the ability to display 3D graphics and HD video and works with Windows 7 system to let you use your multi-touch screen on web pages.

⇨

It has security settings that you can customize, parental controls to stop unwanted downloads and anti-malware to help stop viruses and worms from infecting your computer.

Privacy

Firefox has privacy settings to help you protect your data. This lets you choose whether to browse privately, to remember or clear your browser history or whether or not to allow cookies. This is a very useful tool and can help protect you from spyware.

Checking out web pages

Firefox has a very useful feature that lets you check out web pages. All you do is click on the web page in the address bar then a window opens up telling you about the web page. The screenshot below shows the information it holds on Wikipedia.

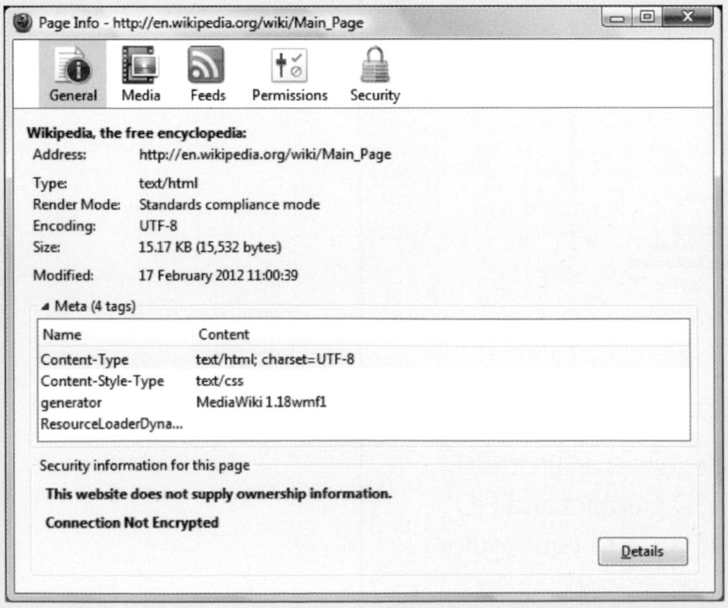

Mobile Firefox

There is even a version for your mobile phone and for a tablet, and sync feature that lets your phone, tablet and computer synchronise, and share and swap data.

Inspect the HTML code on a web page

If you are developing a website then you can use Firefox's Page Inspector, which lets you look into a page's structure and layout as well as view the HTML. The screenshot below shows an example of the HTML language used to create a part of the BBC home page that Firefox has displayed.

```
div#blq-    div#h4di    div#pan    div#pan    div#dz-g    div.pane    div#h1al    h3    a    div.img-    >    HTML    Style    ×

    <a href="http://www.bbc.co.uk/sport/0/football/17070220">
        Man City report chanting in Porto
        <img width="229" height="129" alt="Yaya Toure and Sergio Aguero" src="http://static.bbc.co.uk/h4discoveryzone/ic/newsimg/media
        /images/229/129/58548000/jpg/_58548423_yaya_toure_getty.jpg">
        <div class="img-mask" style="width: 229px; height: 129px; opacity: 0; display: block;"></div>
    </a>
```

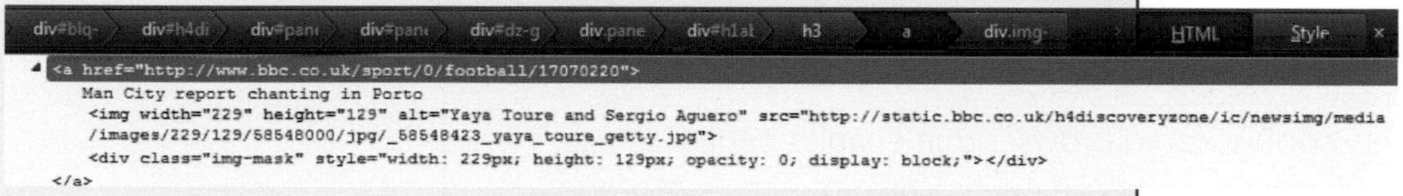

Use of Constructs

Firefox uses *string variables* to hold and display text. For example, when it displays its name this will be stored in the program as a string variable.

Mozilla Firefox Web Browser –

If you change the size of the cache memory then it will store the number as an *integer variable* and represent it in the computer's memory as a binary number.

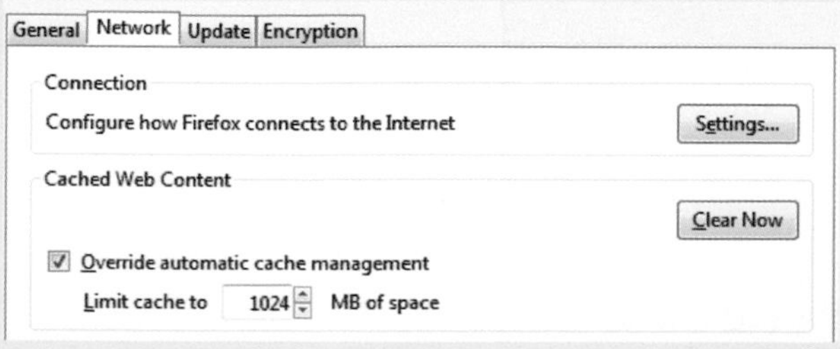

General	Network	Update	Encryption

Connection

Configure how Firefox connects to the Internet   [Settings...]

Cached Web Content

        [Clear Now]

☑ Override automatic cache management

    Limit cache to   [1024 ▲▼]   MB of space

⇒

Firefox uses checkboxes, just like those you can use in Visual Basic, when asking the user to make a *selection*. For example, it uses checkboxes to let the user choose one of the security options or choose to use a master password.

Options							
General	Tabs	Content	Applications	Privacy	Security	Sync	Advanced

☑ Warn me when sites try to install add-ons   Exceptions...

☑ Block reported attack sites
☑ Block reported web forgeries

Passwords

☐ Remember passwords for sites   Exceptions...
☐ Use a master password   Change Master Password...

Saved Passwords...

OK   Cancel   Help

The impact of Firefox on society

Firefox is a very sophisticated browser that enables people to use the Internet's features quickly and safely. With so many safety and privacy concerns regarding the Internet, it is important that browsers have lots of quality safety aspects built into them. If they do not, it makes it easier for criminals to use flaws in the design of the browser to download malware to your computer and start hacking into your system, stealing data and causing disruption.

Firefox has an excellent range of safety features and even enables you choose the type and level of security you want when using the Internet.

General	Network	Update	Encryption

Protocols

☑ Use SSL 3.0   ☑ Use TLS 1.0

Certificates
When a server requests my personal certificate:

○ Select one automatically   ◉ Ask me every time

View Certificates   Revocation Lists   Validation   Security Devices

This means that Firefox provides people with a very safe and efficient tool for using all Internet services. The fact that it is freeware ensures that this safe and efficient software is available to everyone who wants to use it!

Comparing two contemporary software development environments

To complete your National 5 unit you have to compare two contemporary software development environments (programming languages). A good report should contain the following:

1   A comparison between the two languages on how they provide:
   a) Data types: integer, real, string and Boolean variables and arrays.
   b) Standard constructs: *if ... end if, if ... then ... else ... end if, case, fixed loops, loops with conditions*.
   c) Simple conditions: complex conditions using AND, OR, NOT.
2   A comparison of how the two languages represent constructs. For example, are they in text or graphical form? Your report should give suitable examples and consider the relative advantages of each type of representation.
3   A comparison of each language's editing features. You should list the editing features of each language and then make a judgement about the relative advantages of each.
4   A description of how programs in each language are translated. This will involve finding out, for each of the languages, if it is translated using a compiler or a translator. You should then briefly describe how the translator works.

Below is a sample report comparing two programming environments: Truebasic and Kodu.

Example 🚩

Comparison between Truebasic and Kodu
Truebasic

Truebasic is a standard text-based programming language. You can use Truebasic to create a wide range of different types of program. Truebasic provides a standard range of data types such as integer, real, string and Boolean, as well as arrays. It also provides a range of standard programming constructs such as:

- Selection contructs: *if ... end if, if ... then ... else*, case
- Iteration: *fixed loops, conditional loops* with conditions at the beginning of a loop or with conditions at the end of a loop

To enable complex conditions to be set up it provides the logical operators AND, OR, NOT. It also provides a range of predefined functions, such as Len, chr$, Int.

⇨

This example of a Truebasic program illustrates its use of data types and a range of constructs.

```
Let rate = 8.5
Let hours = 45
Call calculate_ overtime((rate),(hours),overtime)
Print "The amount of overtime is £";overtime
Sub calculate_overtime(rate, hours, overtime)
    If hours>40 Then Let hours = hours – 40
Let rate = rate * 1.5
    Let overtime = hours * rate
End Sub
End
```

The programmer has to type in the instructions in the correct logical sequence without breaking the rules of the language (syntax errors) in order to get the game to work.

Truebasic is compiled. When you have finished writing the program and try to run it, it is translated into machine code. If there are any errors they are flagged up at this point.

If there are errors in the program, Truebasic has a range of editing features to help you. It will indicate where the error occurs in the list of instructions and you can cut, copy and paste to amend the instructions.

Kodu

Kodu is completely different. Kodu is designed for one purpose: creating games.

Kodu doesn't have the constructs that a standard programming environment like Truebasic has, but it has a range of conditions and actions which you can select and attach to objects like a rover.

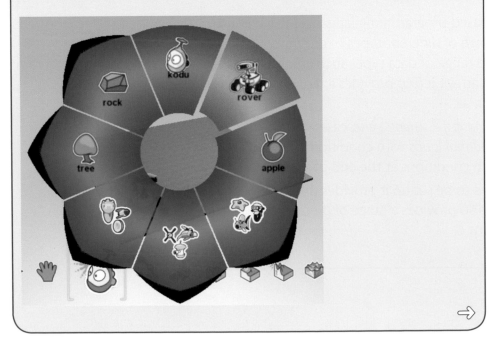

To create a Kodu game you program the computer using graphic-based menus to select objects, their actions and the conditions that control their movement. These menus take the shape of wheels – for example, the wheel below shows a range of conditions which, when they are met, can trigger an action.

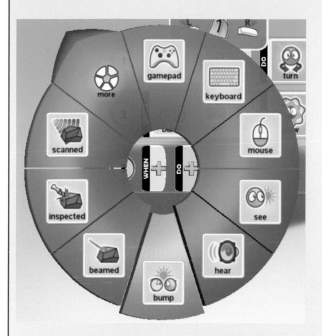

This wheel shows a range of actions.

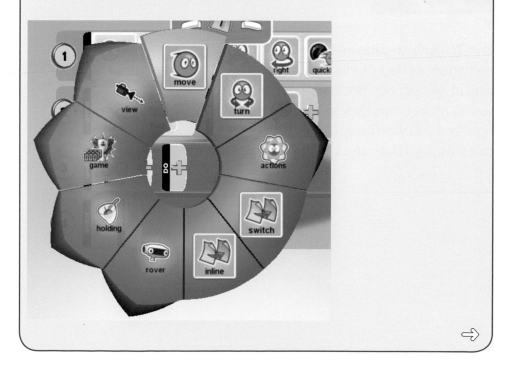

This wheel shows *modifiers* which can affect and direct the action selected.

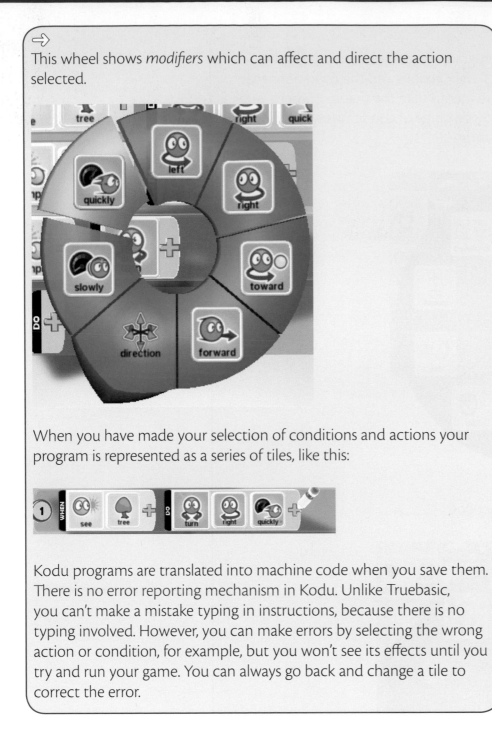

When you have made your selection of conditions and actions your program is represented as a series of tiles, like this:

Kodu programs are translated into machine code when you save them. There is no error reporting mechanism in Kodu. Unlike Truebasic, you can't make a mistake typing in instructions, because there is no typing involved. However, you can make errors by selecting the wrong action or condition, for example, but you won't see its effects until you try and run your game. You can always go back and change a tile to correct the error.

Unit 2 Information System Design and Development

Creating an Information System

Creating an information system using a database

You can create an information system using an application like FileMaker Pro, Microsoft Access or Open Office Base.

Key points !

Your information system will consist of a file, records and fields.

❋ **File**
   Data is stored in files. Files are made up of sets of records.

❋ **Record**
   A record is all the information about one thing in the file, for example one car in a car database. It is made up of a set of fields, for example the name, colour and registration number of a car. An example is shown in the figure below.

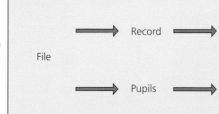

File → Record → Field / Field / Field / Field

File → Pupils → Forename / Surname / Class / Date of birth

❋ **Field**
   A field holds a single item of data in the database, for example a field for the registration number of a car.

Create fields

To define, or set up, new fields in a record you need to plan exactly what information you want to hold on your data subjects. You may need to decide on the field names, field types and field sizes.

Field types

There are many types of field. You need to know about:
- numeric fields, which hold numbers, for example exam marks
- text fields, which hold words, for example forenames of pupils
- graphic fields, which hold images, for example photographs

- date fields, which hold dates, for example date of birth
- time fields, which hold times, for example the start time of an exam
- calculated fields, which hold a formula to calculate, for example averages or totals
- Boolean fields, which are designed to store a value of 1 or 0. Users are commonly presented with a yes/no option
- link fields, which are used for storing links to files on:
  - your computer
  - a network
  - the Internet.

Object (OLE) field

In Microsoft Access, for example, an object field can hold a Word document, an Excel spreadsheet or a Paint graphic.

Primary key

A primary key uniquely identifies each record in a database – for example, a primary key could be an ID number or an account number.

Foreign key

Foreign keys enable you to set up relationships, or links, between tables in a database. For example, an ID number might be used to link two tables.

Validation

Validation is the process of checking that data entered into a system is of the correct type and structure.

You need to know about the following types of validation:
- **Presence check**: this simply checks that the data has been entered and that the data field has not been left blank.
- **Restricted choice**: this type of validation presents the user with a choice, such as a dropdown menu with a range of numbers or text-based items to choose from.
- **Field length check**: this specifies the size of a field, for example stating the number of characters a field can hold.
- **Field range check**: this specifies the range of numbers a field can hold, for example > 0 and < 100.

Avoiding duplication of data

A well-designed database should avoid duplicating data. An efficient design should use foreign keys to link to data already held in a table in the database and avoid the need for re-entry and duplication.

Key points ❗

Database structure

Flat file

A simple database structure has one table containing all the fields and the data they contain. ⇨

⇨

Linked tables

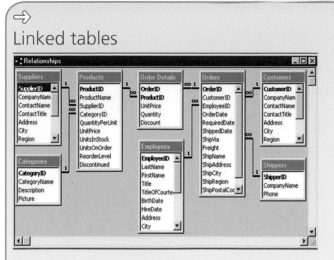

The screenshot above shows a more complex structure that is composed of a range of tables that are linked together to provide the user with different pathways through the database.

Once you have created your information system using a database you can use it to carry out the following operations:

- **Adding records** – A new record can be added to a file when, for example, a new car comes onto the market.
- **Simple search** (a search on one field) – A search is also called *query* or a *find*. A simple search on the database file involves searching on one field only, for example search for those records where the first_name field = "Jack".
- **Sort on one field** – You can arrange, or sort, the records into order based on the contents of one field, for example sort on the second_name field in ascending order (from 'a' to 'z').
- **Complex search** (a search on more than one field) – A complex search is based on two or more fields, for example search for those records where the first_name field = "Jean" AND the second_name field = "Brown".
- **Sort on more than one field** – This is where two or more fields are used to arrange the data, for example sort class file on grade field and second_name field, both in ascending order. This will sort the records so that the grades are in order, with all those with grade 1 followed by grade 2, etc, and each of these groups is sorted into alphabetical order of second name/surname. The screenshot below shows an example of this.

Questions ?

1 What is a file made up of?
2 List the types of fields you can have in your database.
3 Explain why you would include:
   a) a Boolean field
   b) a link field.
4 What is the purpose of a primary field?

Grade	Surname
1	Carrick
1	Dorward
1	Howard
1	Thomson
2	Campbell
2	McCulloch
2	Robertson
2	Shearer

Creating an information system using web authoring software

Web pages are multimedia documents that can hold text, graphics, sound files, animations and video clips.

URL

Every web page has a unique address called a universal resource locator (URL), for example http://www.bbc.co.uk. The URL is divided into three parts:

99

1   The first part is the protocol. The most common one is *http*. This stands for *Hypertext Transfer Protocol*. It is used in transferring web pages to your computer. Some URLs begin with ftp. This stands for *File Transfer Protocol* and is used to transfer files across the Internet.

2   The second part indicates which server the web page is stored on, for example in this case www.bbc.

3   The third part indicates the type of organisation that is storing the web pages, so it would be .co.uk for a company in the UK. Here are some examples of the third part of the URL:

Third part	Type of organisation
.sch	school
.com	commercial company
.net	network organisation
.mil	military
.org	organisation such as a charity
.gov	government organisation
.ac	academic organisation such as a university or college

Hyperlinks

Web pages are linked together by setting up hyperlinks. Setting up a hyperlink is straightforward: you simply choose the section that you want to link from and then insert a hyperlink using the menus. The package will then ask you to browse and point to the page you want to link to. You can choose a range of objects to link the user to the next page, for example a piece of text or a graphic.

Text link	Graphic link
Click here to open the presentation	Click on the graphic to open the presentation

This can be done by using hyperlinks that can be organised into menus, making it easier for the user to get to key menus and to the home page.

Internal hyperlinks

An internal hyperlink is one that takes the user to a new location within the current open web page or website.

External hyperlinks

An external hyperlink is one that opens a web page located on a remote computer.

An external hyperlink reference will include the full address of the remote resource using the URL, for example, http://www.metoffice.gov.uk/public/weather/forecast/glasgow.

You can link your website to another site by setting up an external hyperlink. In this example there are hyperlinks from a music website to other websites related to T in the Park.

Related links

Official website of T in the Park
T in the Park article on Wikipedia
T in the Park at NME.com
T in the Park at The Skinny
T in the Park at The List
T in the Park at STV
T in the Park at The Scotsman
BBC Scotland

An **absolute** web address specifies exactly on which server the web page is stored and directs you to that server. Absolute paths *always* include the domain name of the website, including http://www. – this points to the server on which it is stored. The two addresses below are examples of this:

http://www.bbc.co.uk/sport/football/scottish-premier

http://www.mysite.com/help/articles/how-do-i-set-up-a-webpage.html

On the other hand, a **relative** web address links a web page to other web pages on a single website (using internal hyperlinks). Relative links only point to a file or a file path, often on the computer on which it is being developed. This is often used when developers construct a site in one place and then publish it to another place. An example of this is:

help/articles/how-do-i-set-up-a-webpage.html

Web design

A well-designed website should be easy to navigate and have a well-designed interface which is simple to use and accessible to everyone. To the right is a simple checklist which will help you check the **usability** of a website.

Here is a checklist of some of the things you need to consider when assessing **accessibility**.

- Does the web page have a descriptive title?
- Does the link 'skip to main content' exist?
- Does the website provide any accessibility options, such as 'colour options', 'font re-size options', etc? This might be helpful if your target audience is partially sighted or contains people who are new to the

25-point Website Usability Checklist	
Accessibility	Rating
1. Site load-time is reasonable	✓✓✗
2. Adequate text-to-background contrast	✓✓✗
3. Font size/spacing is easy to read	✓✓✗
4. Flash & add-ons are used sparingly	✓✓✗
5. Images have appropriate ALT tags	✓✓✗
6. Site has custom not-found/404 page	✓✓✗
Identity	
7. Company logo is prominently placed	✓✓✗
8. Tagline makes company's purpose clear	✓✓✗
9. Home-page is digestible in 5 seconds	✓✓✗
10. Clear path to company information	✓✓✗
11. Clear path to contact information	✓✓✗
Navigation	
12. Main nagivation is easily identifiable	✓✓✗
13. Navigation labels are clear & concise	✓✓✗
14. Number of buttons/links is reasonable	✓✓✗
15. Company logo is linked to home-page	✓✓✗
16. Links are consistent & easy to identify	✓✓✗
17. Site search is easy to access	✓✓✗
Content	
18. Major headings are clear & descriptive	✓✓✗
19. Critical content is above the 'fold'	✓✓✗
20. Styles & colours are consistent	✓✓✗
21. Emphasis (bold, etc.) is used sparingly	✓✓✗
22. Ads & pop-ups are unobtrusive	✓✓✗
23. Main copy is concise & explanatory	✓✓✗
24. URLs are meaningful & user-friendly	✓✓✗
25. HTML page titles are explanatory	✓✓✗

Internet. Alternatively, a help page with an article on how to use the existing accessibility options within web browsers would be helpful.

- Do all the informative images have appropriate alternate text?
- Does the web page have an appropriate heading structure?
- Does the website have a site map?
- Are acronyms explained clearly?
- Is all the functionality of the web page available via keyboard?
- Do all the links have descriptive screen text? For example, 'click here' or 'read more' links.
- If an audio content is present, are there synchronised captions or is a text transcript available?

For a full accessibility checklist go to this website: www.w3.org/TR/WCAG10/full-checklist.html

What you should know 👍

Navigation

If your website is complex it can be easy for users to get lost. A good information system needs to have a well-designed navigation to help users find their way around the website.

A well-designed navigation system should:

★ have a range of text and graphic-based hyperlinks sprinkled throughout the website to make moving about as flexible as possible
★ have a navigation bar with clear links to different areas in the website
★ have a site map for visitors to the website who may need a little more help that lists all the sections and web pages, as well as a shorter path to the different areas for those who know what they are looking for
★ be consistent throughout the website. This will help users to learn, through repetition, how to get around the website
★ reduce clutter by grouping links into sections
★ group website navigation links into sections, with each section having between five and seven links, to make it easier to read the navigation scheme
★ keep the number of clicks needed to a minimum. A good design will make the pathways through the website clear and simple, not complex. Ideally a couple of clicks should take you where you want to go.

Visit www.webpagemistakes.ca/website-navigation/ for more hints and tips.

Questions ❓

5 Explain the following terms:
   a) URL
   b) hyperlink.
6 What is an external hyperlink?
7 List four aspects of a well-designed navigation system.
8 What is the purpose of a browser?

Browsers

A **browser** is a program that helps you navigate the **World Wide Web**, move between and look at web pages. In a web browser you can enter the address of the page you want to go to or you can click on a **hyperlink**. A browser will remember where pages are, once the address is added to the **favourites**.

A web browser allows the user to:
- find and look at web pages
- navigate between web pages and websites
- move backwards and forwards between web pages using the back and forward buttons.

A web browser can also:
- remember the location of your favourite pages
- remember which pages you have visited using the 'history' function.

Search engines

Search engines are used to look **for** web pages. A **simple search** is a search that contains one item or topic, for example, 'Computer Network LAN'. The search engine will find all the web pages related to that topic and send the results to your computer for your browser to display.

What you should know 👍

User interface design

A key part of creating an information system is to design a user interface.

Target audience

When you are designing an interface for your information system it is important to know as much as possible about the type of user it is being designed for. There are many things to think about such as the users' age, their interests, their lifestyles, their level of experience, knowledge and skills.

    The more information you have about your target audience the better you will be able to design an interface that they will find easy to use.

Different types of users

The success or failure of an information system depends on the extent to which users are satisfied with the interface, as well the output of the system.

If your information system is targeted at a wide range of users, each with a different skill level, then the interface should be flexible enough to accommodate novices and expert users.

Novice or beginner

A novice or beginner needs to have the simplest design features possible built into the interface. The most commonly used functions and outputs should be readily accessible with plenty of feedback, online help and tutorials easily available. This could be done, for example, by using simple toolbars with rows of clear icons, a navigation bar or an easy-to-use search box. The interface should make it as easy as possible for the user to input data, for example by using a touch screen.

Experienced user

One approach is to present the most common options in a menu but allow an experienced user to select/add other options and features. In terms of input, an experienced user would be more likely to interact with the system using a keyboard and mouse to enter commands or keyboard shortcuts.

Age

It is a good idea to take into account the age of the intended users. If the information system is aimed at very young children, for example, then the interface should be very simple, based largely on easily understood icons and with a touch screen for input. An elderly person may well have trouble with their eyesight and so colour balance, text size and style as well as simple instructions and a touch screen will be required.

Key points !

Designing a user interface

A well-designed user interface will pay attention to:

1 **Visual layout**

This means:
- avoiding using inappropriate or gaudy colours
- balancing the colours
- keeping the screen uncluttered
- avoiding using too many animation special effects.

2 **Navigation**

(See also page 102.)

3 **Consistency**

This involves using the same:
- terms throughout
- sounds to alert, for example an input error

⇨

⇨

- mouse action or command to produce the same action
- font and font size
- graphics style and size
- navigation bar in the same location on each web page
- text alignment.

4 **Interactivity**

This involves using:

- feedback to step users through a process or alert them to errors
- hotspots to trigger actions
- clear links with meaningful link text
- interactive animations
- video clips
- sound files
- polls or quizzes.

5 **Readability**

This means paying attention to:

- text size
- font
- colour balance
- use of headings and sub-headings.

Testing links and navigation

When you have implemented your information system you need to test the navigation, including any pathways and links that you have included.

This can be done in several ways:

- By checking that each of the internal and external hyperlinks operate as intended. This can be carried out by members of the development group.
- By asking people outside of the development group to perform a series of tasks on the system and then asking for their feedback on the suitability of the navigation structure.
- By giving the system to a chosen group of end users, letting them use it in any way they see fit and asking for their feedback (beta testing).

Questions ?

9 **a)** Why is an interface needed?

  b) Name two jobs an interface does.

10 Why should you know your target audience before designing a user interface?

11 How would you design an interface suitable for:

  a) young children?

  b) experienced users?

  c) an elderly person?

12 How would you make an interface more interactive?

13 How would you make an interface consistent?

Scripting and Mark-up Languages

Mark-up languages

A mark-up language is a language used to create web pages.

You need to be able to describe how a web page is constructed using HTML tags. HTML is the standard language used to produce web pages. Tags are codes that are used to identify an element in a document like the headings or the main text of a page.

This table sets out the codes you should be familiar with:

TAG	What the TAG identifies
<html>…</html>	Start and end of an HTML file
<head>…</head>	Start and end of the head section
<title>…</title>	Page title
<body>…</body>	Start and end of the content of a page
<hx>… </hx>	Headings numbered 1–6
<I>…</I>	Italics style
…	Boldface style
<center>…</center>	Centre alignment
<p>…</p>	Paragraph

This short example of HTML coding sets out the background colour, text colour, alignment and size.

```
<body bgcolor="#FFFF99">
<p align="center"><b><font color="#0000FF" size="6">Information System
Design and Development</font></b></p>
<div align="center">
```

Activities

1 Set up a simple web page using a selection of the tags in the table above.
2 Print out a screen dump of the page and then print out the HTML coding.

Scripting languages

A script language is a simple programming language that you can use to write scripts. Scripts are small programs that can automate tasks by creating a macro or generating dynamic content for web pages.

There is a range of scripting languages available: VB Script, based on Visual Basic; Applescript, for use with software running on Apple computers; and PHP which is embedded in HTML files to produce dynamic content on web pages.

JavaScript is another very commonly used scripting language that is used:
- to add interactivity to HTML pages
- to create 'cookies' – programs that can help gather information from the computers of visitors to a website
- in PDF documents and desktop widgets.

JavaScript is:
- usually embedded directly into HTML pages
- an example of freeware – you don't need to buy a licence
- an interpreted language
- easy to use. It has many of the standard features of a programming language such as setting up and assigning variables, using repeat loops, using *if* + conditions, using arithmetic and comparator operators.

Here is an example of a simple Javascript that checks the time on your browser and outputs a suitable message:

```
<html>
<body>
<script type="text/javascript">
var d = new Date();
var time = d.getHours();
if (time < 12)
{
document.write("<b>Good morning</b>");
}
else
{
document.write("<b>Good afternoon</b>");
}
</script>
```

If you want to investigate JavaScript more, try this excellent free JavaScript tutorial website: www.w3schools.com/js/

Another example of a scripting language is Visual Basic for Applications (VBA). Here is a VBA to calculate someone's age from their date of birth held in a database.

```
PFunction Age(varDOB As Variant, Optional varAsOf As Variant) As Variant
    ' Purpose: Return the Age in years
    ' Arguments: varDOB = Date Of Birth
        ' varAsOf = the date to calculate the age at, or today if missing
    ' Return: Whole number of years
    Dim dtDOB As Date
    Dim dtAsOf As Date
    Dim dtBDay As Date ' Birthday in the year of calculation
        Age = Null ' Initialize to Null
    ' Validate parameters
    If IsDate(varDOB) Then
        dtDOB = varDOB
        If Not IsDate(varAsOf) Then ' Date to calculate age from
            dtAsOf = Date
        Else
            dtAsOf = varAsOf
        End If
    If dtAsOf >= dtDOB Then ' Calculate only if it is after person was
    born
        dtBDay = DateSerial(Year(dtAsOf), Month(dtDOB), Day(dtDOB))
            Age = DateDiff("yyyy", dtDOB, dtAsOf) + (dtBDay > dtAsOf)
        End If
    End If
End Function
```

Most general-purpose packages, including databases, have some sort of
scripting or macro capability.

Questions ?

1 What is the purpose of a mark-up language?
2 Write out some HTML that you have written.
3 What is a script?
4 List three scripting languages.
5 What is JavaScript used for?
6 Write out an example of a script you have written.

Adding Text, Graphics, Sound and Video

> **What you should know** 👍
>
> ## Text, graphics, sound and video
>
> Information systems can hold the following types of data:
> - ★ Text: characters, words, paragraphs
> - ★ Graphics: drawings, cartoons, photographs, graphs, designs
> - ★ Sound: music tracks, voice-overs
> - ★ Video: clips taken by digital camcorder or downloaded from the Internet

Compressing graphics

Bit mapped graphic files can be very large indeed and demand lots of storage space as well as taking up time when transmitting across a network.

The factors that control how large a graphic file is are:
- the size/dimensions of the graphic
- the resolution
- the bit depth.

When processing graphic data we can choose to vary the *resolution* and the *colour depth* as well as use different levels of lossy compression.

However, a trade-off between file size and image quality is involved in using each of these compression methods.

Increasing levels of compression

JPEG files can vary in their level of compression. The higher the level of compression, the smaller the file size. The smaller the file size, the more data is lost and the poorer the graphic quality is.

Changing the resolution

The resolution is the number of pixels used to represent a graphic, for example 300 × 300 pixels per inch. Increasing the resolution (having more pixels) increases the size of the file and produces a higher quality graphic.

Increasing the colour depth

The colour depth is the number of bits used to represent the colour of each pixel in a graphic. As the colour depth increases, so does the size of the file.

Look carefully at the examples in the following tables.

Colour depth	No. of possible colours per pixel	File size for a bit map 3 inches × 3 inches at a resolution of 600 pixels per inch
1 bit	2, black or white	405000 bytes = 395.5 Kilobytes
8 bit	256 colours	3240000 bytes = 3.08 Megabytes

Resolution	Pixels per 6-inch square graphic	No. of Bytes representing each pixel	No. of colours available	File size in Bytes	File size in Megabytes
600 × 600	12,960,000	1 Byte	256	12,960,000	12.36
600 × 600	12,960,000	2 Bytes	65536	25,920,000	24.72
600 × 600	12,960,000	3 Bytes	16,777,216	38,800,000	37.8

An A4 page bit map, with a resolution of 600 × 600 and 24-bit colour depth would take 90.63 Megabytes of storage space.

What you should know

Formats for storing graphic files

BMP

* The BMP (bit map) format stores colour data for each pixel in the image without any compression and so, as the table above shows, .bmp files can be very large indeed.

GIF

* The GIF file format uses lossless compression to reduce the file size without losing any of the data about the image. It does this by using a code to store patterns of bits that occur repeatedly throughout a graphic file.
* GIF is based on an 8-bit colour code giving a maximum of 2^8, 256, colours. A maximum of 256 colours means that GIFs are unsuitable for storing photographic images and are therefore used to represent charts, cartoons, or drawings.

JPEG

* The JPEG is a bit map graphic file format that uses lossy compression. This makes the graphic file smaller by cutting out parts of the graphic that won't be noticed by the human eye.
* It is often used when storing digital photographs.
* It is not used for storing cartoons or drawings because some of the data that is lost in these types of image would be noticed and this reduces the quality of the image.

PNG

* PNG uses lossless com pression.
* It achieves 5–25 per cent more compression than GIF format.
* It can have a bit depth of up to 48 bits = range of 2^{48} colours.
* It enables control over the degree of transparency of a graphic.

Questions

1 Calculate the storage requirements of a graphic 4 inch × 4 inch with a resolution of 300 × 300 pixels and a bit depth of:
a) 8 bits
b) 24 bits.

Questions

2 Why is a GIF not suitable for storing photographic images?
3 Name the type of compression that GIFs and PNG files have in common.
4 Describe the type of compression that JPEG files use.

Compressing sound files

Why compress sound files? The simple answer is that they can be very large files.

You can use this formula to calculate the size of a sound file:

File size = sampling frequency × sound time × sampling depth × number of channels

- *Sampling depth*, also called sample resolution, is the number of bits, or bytes, used to store a single sample. The greater the sample depth, the more detailed the digital picture of the original sound will be. However, a high sample depth could mean a very large file. The diagram below shows a low sample depth: the sound wave on the right does not look much like the original sound on the left. If the blocks were to be made narrower we would get a picture that was much closer to the original wave. WAV files are sampled using a bit depth of 8 or 16 bits.

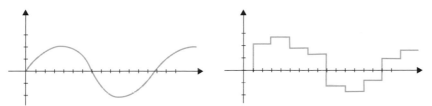

- *Sampling frequency* is how often the sound is sampled in a second. It is measured in Hertz (Hz), or more usually kilohertz (KHz). Standard sampling rates are 44.1 KHz, 22.05 KHz or 11.025 KHz. The more often you sample, the better the sound quality, but the file size is larger as a result.
- *Sound time* is the duration of the clip in seconds. Obviously longer tracks take up more space!
- *Number of channels*, for example, whether it is mono or stereo.

Higher bit rate, sampling frequency, sound time and number of channels = higher sound quality + larger file size.

What you should know 👍

Formats for storing sound files

WAV
WAV is the standard for storing sound files on Windows systems and can be sampled at a bit depth of either 8 bits or 16 bits. It uses one of the following sampling rates: 11.025 KHz, 22.05 KHz or 44.1 KHz. Wav files can be very large. One minute of sound can take up as much as 27 Megabytes of storage.

MP3
MP3 is a format for compressing sounds which uses a lossy technique that does not seriously degrade the quality of the sound because it filters out parts of the original sound that the human ear cannot

⇒

detect. After filtering it applies further compression techniques. One minute of music takes up around 1 Megabyte of space.

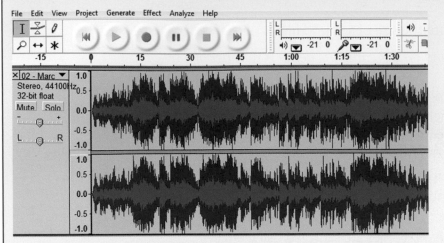

The quality and size of an MP3 file depends on the bit rate used when the file is compressed. The bit rate is a measure of the number of bits sent in one second to transmit a sound file. The bit rate range of an MP3 file is 96 to 320 kilobytes per second. Higher bit rate = a better quality sound + a larger file size.

Questions ?

5 Explain why sound files need to be compressed.
6 Explain the terms *sampling frequency* and *sampling depth*.
7 Describe the differences between an MP3 file and a WAV file.

Compressing video files

Video files can be the largest of them all. How can you calculate the size of a video file? You can use this formula:

File size = length of a clip in seconds × frame rate × bit depth × resolution

- The *length* of the clip in seconds is obviously a factor.
- The number of *frames per second* (fps), also called the *frame rate*, is very important in terms of both quality and file size. If the frame rate is set too low the action appears jerky, if it is too high then the amount of data to be stored is very large and the processor and/or graphics card will have to do a lot more work. Professional video is captured at 25 fps, cinema is 24 fps, and web cams are usually set at around 8 or 16 fps.
- The number of colours available affects the size of each frame. The technical term is the *colour depth*, or often the *bit depth*. This is the same as for bit mapped images, with a number of bits or bytes needed to store each pixel. A typical range would be 8-bit colour, giving 256 possible colours, up to 32-bit colour with 4 billion colours.
- The *resolution* of the image, measured in dots per inch (dpi), also affects the size of each frame and therefore the size of the clip. If the resolution is too low the video will be grainy. If it is set higher the clip will be of higher quality but will be very large. The resolution is often given as the screen dimensions in pixels, i.e. standard PAL video resolution is 768 × 576; this sum gives the number of pixels per frame.

Example

What is the uncompressed file size of a 30-second video clip, taken at 25 frames per second (fps)? The resolution is 640 × 480 and the video was shot in 24-bit colour.

Frame size = 640 × 480 × 24 = 7372800 bits = 921600 bytes

1 second clip = 921600 × 25 = 23040000 bytes = 22500 Kb

30 second clip = 22500 × 30 = 675000 Kb = 659.2 Mb

What you should know

Formats for storing video files

AVI

The Audio Video Interleave (AVI) format was developed by Microsoft and is commonly used in Windows applications like Media Player. This format does not have built-in compression. The maximum resolution is 320 × 240, with a maximum frame rate of 30 fps. The main problem with this format is the limit on the size of the video file which is 2 Gigabytes. This is being replaced by the Windows Media Video (WMV) format, as this does support compression.

MPEG

The Moving Picture Experts Group (MPEG) format is one of the most common formats for video. MPEG-2 is the standard for DVDs and can compress a two-hour video into a few Gigabytes. Do the sums to see how good that is! The MP3 audio format is a spin-off from this as it is the soundtrack layer (layer 3) from this format. The fourth 'edition' of this format, MPEG-4, was launched in 1997 and allows variable data rates. This means that the format can be used in high-end TV or for sending pictures to your mobile!

MPEG-4

* is a compression method specially designed for low-bandwidth video and audio encoding (less than 1.5 Mb per second).
* can deliver high-quality audio and video over the Internet to desktops, laptops, tablets and smartphones.

Comparison between AVI and MPEG-4

* Both AVI and MPEG-4 are lossy formats which sacrifice quality for file size.
* Both AVI and MPEG-4 can contain both audio and video data in a file container.
* The quality of a video file is not dependent on the type of container file format as it is dependent on the type of codec contained within the container file format.
* H.264 video codec, frequently used with the MPEG-4 container, is thought to be one of the highest-quality video standards available.

Questions ?

8 Using this formula *File size = length of a clip in seconds × frame rate × bit depth × resolution*, explain why video files need to be compressed.

9 Describe the differences between an AVI and an MPEG video file.

Text files

Standard file formats are recognised by all computers. You don't need specific software, hardware or operating systems to use them. Using standard file formats, you can be sure that your text files are very portable and can be transferred easily from one package to another.

What you should know 👍

Text (.txt)

A .txt file has none of the information about the formatting of the document such as the text style, alignment, etc. As it lacks the formatting information, a .txt file is more compact than a Rich Text file, demands less storage space and is quicker to transmit across a network.

It will also be recognised by any text editing or word processing program and can also be processed by most other software programs.

Rich Text Format (RTF)

A file saved in RTF has all the formatting information that the .txt file lacks, as well as the actual text. It includes all the information about styles, fonts, sizes, paragraphing and indentation.

PDF

PDF stands for Portable Document Format; Adobe Systems developed PDF files. It is mainly used for sharing and publishing documents across the Internet. To create or view a PDF file you can use any suitable software, for example Adobe Acrobat or Foxit Reader.

Questions ❓

10 What is the advantage of saving a file in .txt format?
11 What is the advantage of saving a file in .rtf format?
12 What is the advantage of saving a file in .pdf format?

Chapter 9

Hardware

An essential part of designing an information system is the selection of suitable hardware.

What you should know 👍

Main memory

Main memory can be either RAM or ROM.

RAM: Random Access Memory

* The processor can write to, or read from, RAM at high speed.
* Data held in RAM can be changed.
* All data in RAM is lost when the power is switched off.
* RAM is the working space of the computer. It holds all of the programs and data files currently in use.

ROM: Read Only Memory

* Data is stored permanently in ROM; it is not lost when the power goes off.
* Data in the ROM cannot be changed.
* ROM holds vital systems data and programs.

N4

The processor

The processor is the 'brain' of the computer and deals with all the movement of data and any calculations to be carried out. A processor is made of silicon crystal wavers, which hold millions of tiny electronic components.

Clock speed

Clock speeds are a measure of how powerful a processor is, for example 3GHz clock speeds are measured in Megahertz (MHz) or Gigahertz (GHz). 1 MHz = 1 million pulses per second; 1 GHz = 1000 million pulses per second.

The clock pulses, measured in GHz, regulate and coordinate the activities in the processor.

Processor types

Multiple core processors

These have two or more processors working together to make the system work better. For example, there are duo-processors, with two or more processors working together, quad processors, with four processors working together and even hex-core processors with six processors.

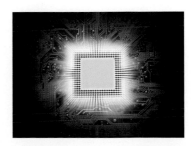

Low power processors

These have lower clock speeds and use less electricity. They are used in laptops, netbooks, mobile phones, MP3 players, tablet computers and games consoles.

For further information on multiple core and low power processers, check out http://tinyurl.com/y3sblo7

Key points !

Measuring the size of memory

We use these terms when measuring computer's memory.

Bit	Binary digit: a single 1 or 0
Byte	8 Bits, for example 11001110
Kilobyte	1024 Bytes
Megabyte	1024 Kilobytes
Gigabyte	1024 Megabytes
Terabyte	1024 Gigabytes

Questions ?

1   What is the purpose of a processor?
2   When the system is switched off, what happens to the data held in
    a) RAM?
    b) ROM?
3   What is a processor's clock speed measured in?
4   Give the clock speed of a low power Intel Atom processor.
5   How many megabytes of data can be stored on a 120 Gigabyte hard disk?

N4

Backing storage

Hard disk

This is a metal disk with magnetised surfaces on which data is stored as patterns of magnetic spots. The disks are in sealed units to stop dust and dirt corrupting data. They are usually fixed in the computer, but you can get portable external drives.

Advantages

- Fast access times, direct access
- Fast data transfer rates
- Cheap per megabyte

USB flash drive

The most common form of portable backing storage is the USB flash drive.

Also called pen drive or memory stick, the flash drive shown in the photograph on the right is a small portable backing storage device with no moving parts. Flash drives can store large amounts of data, up to 512 Gb. They simply plug into the USB ports on your computer and are a convenient way of making backups and of transferring data between computers.

Optical storage

Optical storage is the use of laser technology to store data. The following describes the different types of optical storage that are in use today.

CD-ROM

A CD-ROM, shown in the photograph on the right, is an example of optical storage. CD-ROM stands for *Compact Disk – Read Only Memory*. It is fast and can store up to 700 Mb of data. It cannot be written to – the data is fixed at the time of manufacture. The data is read by a sensor that detects laser light reflected from the surface of the disk. The speed of a CD drive is given as a number, for example 52X (52 × 150 Kilobits per second).

CD-R

This is CD-recordable – it allows you to record data *once*. Once data is recorded on it, it works just like a CD-ROM. It is read only. It can hold 700 Mb. The speed of a CD-R drive is given as two numbers, the read speed and the write speed.

CD-RW

This is CD-rewriteable so you can record data over and over again, just like hard disks. You can use them to make backups of large files, for example groups of photos, and you can change the data stored on the disk as often as you want. A CD-RW drive has three speeds: one for writing data, one for rewriting and one for reading, for example Write 52X, Rewrite 24X and Read 52X.

DVD-ROM

A DVD-ROM uses optical technology to read data. Like a CD-ROM it is read only. A DVD-ROM has much larger data capacity than a CD-ROM. Single-sided single layered DVDs have a capacity of 4.7 Gb. Double-sided, multi-layered DVDs have a capacity of 17 Gb. The speed of a DVD-ROM drive is given as a number, for example 16X. This is different from a CD, as each 1X is 1250 Kilobits per second.

DVD-R

DVD-recordable allows you to record data once. After recording the data cannot be changed. They have the same capacity as DVDs but a DVD-R drive has two speeds, one for writing and one for reading data, for example Write 6X, Read 12X.

DVD-RW

This is a DVD that allows you to record data over and over again (see photograph on the right). Like hard disks, you can use them to make backups of very large files, such as home movies from your digital video camera, and you can change the data stored on the disk as often as you want.

A DVD-RW drive has three speeds: one for writing data, one for rewriting and one for reading, for example Write 6X, Rewrite 2.4X and Read 12X.

Questions ?

6 Describe two key differences between backing storage and RAM.
7 Describe the difference in capacity between a CD-ROM and a DVD-ROM.
8 What is a USB flash drive used for?
9 Why would you use an external hard drive?

Input devices

Keyboard

Keyboards, as shown in the photograph on the right, are useful input devices and are used for typing in data and commands.

Mouse

A mouse lets the user interact with the computer system. The hand-sized case of the mouse has at least one button on top and (usually) a laser fitted underneath. Sensors detect the movement of the mouse relative to the surface underneath. The mouse is used to control the cursor on the screen and to manipulate icons and menus.

Microphone

A microphone is used to input sound data, for example when recording a voice-over. It is also used by voice-recognition systems, which allow the user to give commands to the computer by speaking.

Touchpad

This is a small pad, usually found on laptops, with sensors that detect the movements and taps of your finger. This lets the user control the position of the cursor on the screen and select icons and open menus. Touchpads are more convenient when using a laptop in places where it is difficult to use a mouse.

Digital camera

This is a camera for taking digital pictures (see photograph on the right). The quality is measured in megapixels: the number of millions of detectors in the grid that detects the picture. A reasonably good one will be 16 megapixels and will cost less than £80. Advantages: they can hold lots of images without film, you can delete the pictures you don't want, you can transfer them to a computer and print them out easily.

Joystick/Joypad

Joysticks or joypads (see photograph on the right) are used mainly in games to give the user control over the game objects like a car, a plane or a human character. Controlling a game using a joystick or joypad is much easier than using the keyboard and mouse.

Graphics tablet

A graphics tablet (as shown in the photograph on the right) is a flat pad with electronic sensors below the surface. These detect the movements of a pointing device (stylus) and move the cursor on the screen accordingly. This system has the advantage of being very sensitive and accurate and is used in engineering and design

(N4) systems.

Scanner

A scanner enables the user to capture images, like photos or documents, onto the computer in a digital form (see photograph on the right). The scanner works by shining a light on the document and reading where the light reflects, i.e. the white bits. This information is changed into binary values for light and dark and saves the file.

Webcam

Webcams are digital cameras that are used to take photographs (see photograph on the right). The photographs are then transferred to a web page and then sent across the Internet. They are used in a number of ways, for example to view traffic flowing along motorways and to advertise tourist attractions and business sites.

Questions ?

10 Which input devices are used to
   a) control a game?
   b) control a cursor on a laptop?
   c) capture and send pictures across the Internet?
   d) capture sound?

Output devices
LCD and TFT screens
Liquid Crystal Display (LCD)

LCD screens use transistors and a thin film of liquid crystals to control the light passing through the screen (see photograph on the right). They are found on palmtops and laptops, smartphones and tablets because they are light, compact, need little power and can be run on batteries. One problem is that some LCD screens are not very bright and can cause eye strain if they are used for too long.

Thin Film Transistor (TFT)

TFT is a type of LCD screen that uses lots of transistors to produce a high quality display. A TFT screen can display animations and three-dimensional graphics much more clearly than ordinary LCD screens (see photograph on the right). The disadvantage is that they can be a lot more expensive than ordinary LCD screens.

On desktop computers TFT screens are used because they take up less space on a desk than CRT (cathode ray tube) monitors and are less awkward to move around.

(N4)

Key points !

How to compare monitors

You compare monitors using resolution and cost.

Resolution	This determines the quality of images that can be displayed.	For example, a 1680 × 1050 high resolution screen or a 1280 × 1024 medium resolution screen.
Cost	What you have to pay!	This varies all the time.

Activities

1 Use the Internet to get the latest information on monitors: check, where appropriate, for resolution and cost.

Inkjet printer

An inkjet printer sprays ink onto paper to form letters and pictures (see photograph on the right). It produces high quality output and is less expensive to buy than a laser printer. However, running costs can be high as the toner is expensive (and it dries out if you don't use it often). They are also a lot slower than laser printers.

Laser printer

A laser printer works by using a laser beam to put the image of a page onto a photosensitive drum. The toner or ink then sticks to the charged drum. This is then transferred to paper and fused by heat to make it stick. They are very fast and produce very high quality output. However, they can be more expensive to buy than an inkjet. (See photograph on the right.)

Key points !

How to compare printers

You compare printers using the following criteria:

Speed	This is measured in pages per minute (ppm), for example 8 ppm.
Resolution	The higher the resolution, the more dots per inch (dpi), the better the quality of the printout. Printouts from a printer capable of 900 dpi will be poorer in quality than those from a 1200 dpi printer.
Cost	Capital cost: the initial cost of buying the printer. Running costs: the cost of toner or ink (and paper).

Activities

2 Use the Internet to get the latest information on printers: check for speed, resolution and cost.

Questions ?

11 Use the Internet to find an example of a colour laser printer. Write down the speed, resolution and cost.
12 Use the Internet to find an example of a TFT high resolution screen.

Types of computer

Supercomputer

Supercomputers have thousands of processors and very large memory capacity which is measured in terabytes. They are very powerful and are used for tasks that need lots of very high speed calculations, such as scientific research, medical research, forecasting the weather and modelling climate change.

Desktop computer

A desktop computer consists of a monitor, keyboard, mouse, processor, main memory and the hard disk drive, CD and DVD drives (see photograph on the right). They are reasonably compact and fit onto a workstation or desk.

Laptop computer

A laptop:

- is small enough to use on your lap comfortably
- is useful for working away from the home or office
- is light, weighing less than 4kg, and can be carried easily
- is powered by batteries (or by mains adapter)
- has an LCD or TFT screen
- has a standard keyboard and a touchpad as well as a range of disk drives.

Tablet

A tablet is a mobile computer with:

- a flat touch screen usually between 7 and 10 inches in size
- a screen resolution commonly around 1200×800
- a processor with a speed around 1.5 GHz
- memory capacity between 16 and 64 Gb
- a battery with a life of around 10 hours before recharging
- an Internet connection.

 **Activities**

3 Check out: www.tabletpccomparison.net/

Smartphone

A smartphone:

- is a mobile phone with a memory to hold an address book and ring tones; and the ability to send, receive and store text messages
- is a multimedia device that can handle text, graphics, audio and video
- has a browser to access web pages and send email
- has a digital camera to capture images and send them through the phone network and the Internet
- can play MP3 files and games
- can connect with laptops and desktops.

What is an interface?

The interface is the combination of hardware and software needed to enable the processor in a computer to communicate with the external devices. You need an interface to connect your computer to external devices like a printer or an external hard drive or USB flash drive.

What does an interface do?

An interface will do jobs like:

- change electrical voltages
- deal with control signals
- change analogue data to digital form
- store incoming data so that the processor can get on with other tasks.

What you should know 👍

You should know about a range of common interfaces. The table below will help you.

Type	Speed
USB 2.0	480 megabits per second
Firewire 800	up to 800 Megabits per second
Express Card	up to 2.5 Gigabits per second
USB 3.0	up to 5 Gigabits per second
SATA	up to 6 Gigabits per second
Thunderbolt	up to 10 Gigabits per second per channel

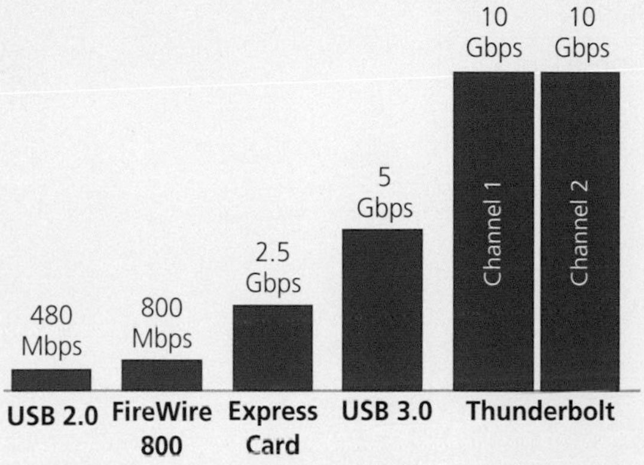

Activities ✏️

4 Update your knowledge by using the Internet to get information about the latest interfaces being developed.

Questions ?

13 Describe two differences between a laptop and a desktop.
14 List two key features of a supercomputer.
15 Describe three features of a smartphone.
16 Describe the screen size, processor speed and memory capacity of a tablet computer.

Operating systems

An operating system (OS) is a program, or set of programs, that controls all the tasks a computer carries out. Without the operating system no other tasks could take place.

Operating systems carry out important functions on the computer. They:
● manage the use of both the internal memory and the backing storage
● manage the files and keep track of where they are stored in the system

123

- provide the user with an interface, usually a graphics-based interface, increasingly with a touch screen and even voice input
- run other software
- control the use of devices such as printers.

Here is a list of common operating systems:

Personal operating systems	Workgroup operating systems (for small LANs in homes, schools and small businesses)	Enterprise operating systems (for large businesses and organisations)
Microsoft Windows 7, Windows Phone	XP Professional Microsoft Windows Server 2011	Microsoft Windows Server 2008
Mac OSX Lion	Mac OSX Lion	Mac OSX Lion
Linux	Linux Ubuntu	Red Hat Enterprise Linux

Activities

5 Use the Internet to find out about the latest operating systems.

Questions ?

17 List four functions of an operating system.
18 Describe the operating system used
   a) in your school
   b) at home.

Networking

Stand alone computers

Computers can be used on their own without being connected to a network, but all computers now have the capability to connect with a network.

Local Area Network (LAN)

A Local Area Network (LAN) is a small network in a single room, building or site. Examples are a school network, a network in an office, or connecting your computers together to play games at home. The computers can be linked using copper cables or by a wireless connection.

Wireless networking

Wireless networks use radio waves, microwaves or infrared light to transmit data. All you need is a transmitter/receiver in every machine and a central device, such as a wireless router, to pass the data around the network.

Any modern computer can be fitted with a wireless network card, sometimes by just plugging it into the USB slot.

Advantages

Wireless networks are easy to install, as there is no need for cables. Also, you can move around when you work without trailing wires. They have reasonably fast transmission speeds, although they can be slower than physical cables. The main problem is that they are very vulnerable to hackers, who can just 'tap in' to your signal. You need to take care when setting up network security if you don't want others to access your files or use your Internet connection.

Key points (!)

Wired networks

Here is some information on the types of wiring used on LAN.

Name	Description
Twisted pair	This cable consists of two copper wires twisted around each other. It is widely used because it is cheap and capable of transmitting data quickly, at speeds of 100 megabits per second.
Coaxial	This cabling is not so commonly used as it is more expensive. It is used where there is lots of interference that can corrupt data because it has a protective shield to prevent interference.
Fibre-optic	Fibre-optic cable is made up of fine strands of glass that transmit data as pulses of light. Fibre-optic cable transmits at *very* high speeds. It also doesn't lose data because of interference and is very secure. It is very expensive to install.

The Internet

The Internet is a global system of interconnected computer networks. It has a number of different elements:

- The World Wide Web which is made up of multimedia web pages that are stored on computers across the world. Web pages hold text, sounds, graphics, animations and videos. These are linked by hyperlinks.
- Search engines to help users find their way around the Internet.
- Forums and chatrooms where you can meet people and discuss all sorts of topics.

(N4) The Internet has many uses, for example sending email, social networking (Facebook, Twitter), online shopping and banking.

Questions ?

1 What is a LAN?
2 List three places where you would find an LAN.
3 List three features of fibre-optic cable.
4 Describe two advantages of wireless networking.
5 What is the Internet?
6 List three parts of the Internet.

Comparison of local versus 'Cloud'

Businesses now have the choice of buying and installing their own computer hardware and software, and paying for network connections, maintenance and updating; or they can use the 'Cloud'. This means they can rent equipment, software, storage facilities and access to the Internet on a pay-as-you-go basis.

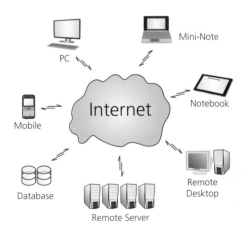

Cloud computing customers:	Local/non-Cloud users:
● do not own the physical infrastructure. The powerful servers that provide the computing power are owned by the Cloud Computing provider.	● own their computers, backing storage and wired or wireless connection equipment.
● can rent storage space on servers. Customers can have a contract that enables them to decide how much storage space they need for their data. This arrangement can be very flexible and customers can easily scale their storage up or down as required.	● own their hard drives, optical storage and servers, which they have to maintain and update.
● can have access to powerful networks without great initial expense. A business does not need to spend large amounts of money buying and installing expensive computer systems and networks in order to access powerful computing resources.	● must bear the initial costs in buying computers, backing storage and software, which can be very high.
● can access a wide range of application software and software for developing applications. As soon as the contract is signed a customer can have instant access to all the software – databases, accounting software, programming software – it needs without having to buy the hardware or pay for and install the software.	● need to pay for and install all the software needed.
● have access to technical support. Technical support is supplied by the Cloud provider as a standard part of their service.	● need to provide/pay for technical support.
● are billed for their service based either on the time they spend using the network or on a monthly or quarterly basis. Payment can be very flexible. A business that only needs to use the Cloud services for short periods of time will be billed according to the hours and minutes spent online. Others will be billed on a regular monthly/quarterly basis.	● must bear the High initial startup costs before the business can begin to use the system.
● may have what is called a hybrid cloud system where important data is stored locally. Security concerns mean that some customers keep what is called 'mission critical data' in computer storage devices in their offices.	● are responsible for their own security. They do not have the worry that data stored in the 'Cloud' will be hacked into.

Comparing peer-to-peer networks and client/server networks

Comparison criteria	Peer-to-peer	Client/server
Constituent elements	This is a network in which the computers are managed independently of each other and have equal status when it comes to communicating with each other, sharing resources like data files and peripherals, or carrying out key operations such as validating users.	This network is composed of a *client*, which is a workstation operated by a user. A *server* is a computer that controls a resource that it makes available to clients on the network. Examples of resources are: data file, printers, applications, access to web pages.

File Server

Client   Client   Client   Client

Sharing resources	In a peer-to-peer mode each workstation can make its resources available to the other workstations on the network. The resources could be, for example, a hard disk, a CD-ROM, a laser printer or data files. A shared resource simply appears as another device (drive or printer) connected to the station and the user accesses the resource transparently.	All resources on the network are managed by the servers which provide access to resources such as data files, printers and web access to the client stations.
Centralised storage	There is no centralised storage, so each workstation stores its data independently.	Data is normally stored on central backing storage attached to a file server.
Backup regime	There is no centralised storage so implementing a rigorous network-wide backup system is very difficult. What often happens is that each workstation backs up its own data independently.	Centralised backing storage means that a rigorous backup regime can be organised with, for example, regular backups being made each day from the file server.
Security	Security is difficult to implement because there is no mechanism for centrally managing access to the network. Individual workstations can set up IDs and passwords.	A server holding a database of user information that contains IDs, passwords and details of users' access privileges is normally given the task of implementing the security mechanisms on the network.
Type of environment	It is best suited to a 'trusting environment', for example in a family home.	It is commonly used in businesses and organisations.

Questions ?

7 Describe how the files are stored
   a) in a local system
   b) using the Cloud.
8 What financial advantage is there in using the Cloud?
9 Describe the security worries people have over the use of the Cloud.
10 How are files stored
   a) on a peer-to-peer network?
   b) on a client server network?
11 What is
   a) a client?
   b) a server?
12 Why is security easier to manage on a client server network?

Security risks

Viruses

A computer virus is a program that makes copies of itself, attaches itself to programs you have installed on your computer, and then damages your system. What are the signs that your computer has a virus? There are lots of them. For example, your hard drive could start spinning for no reason, data could go missing, the screen display could go wrong or the key board may malfunction.

Worms

Similar to a virus, a worm is a program that makes copies of itself and then spreads through a network in order to damage systems as it goes along.

Trojans

This is a program that looks harmless and tricks you into running it on your computer. It then carries out its real task, for example displaying adverts on the desktop or installing unwanted toolbars.

(N4) Hackers and hacking

Hackers are people who try to break into computer systems and steal or corrupt data. The main defence against hacking is to control access to computer systems using a system of IDs and passwords. Other techniques might include encryption of sensitive data or more secure hardware, like dedicated network cables.

Keylogger

A keylogger is a program designed to track and monitor users' keystrokes, and is often used to steal passwords, credit card numbers, etc.

Spyware

Spyware programs gather information about you from your computer. This can be personal information or information about which websites you have visited. Some spyware can also change your computer settings.

Online fraud

Online fraud is the use of the Internet to commit crime. There are lots of types of online fraud. Here is a sample list.

- Account takeover
- Advance fee frauds
- Bank and cheque fraud
- Charity donation fraud
- Clairvoyant or psychic scams
- Government agency scams
- Health scams
- Holiday fraud
- Identity fraud
- Inheritance fraud
- Loan scams
- Lottery scams
- Online shopping fraud
- Work-from-home scams

If you want to find out more, check out this website: www.actionfraud.org.uk/fraud-az-online-fraud

Phishing

Phishing is an attempt to get your personal information such as your bank account details by pretending to be a charity, for example, or

claiming that you have won a cash prize. It is often carried out by email.
Phishing can use keyloggers, trojans, spyware and even ordinary email to
steal your information.

Identity theft

This is when people steal your personal details such as bank account
details and pretend to be you, for example when buying online or
withdrawing money from your bank account. Keyloggers, trojans, spyware
and even ordinary email can be used to steal your identity.

Denial of service

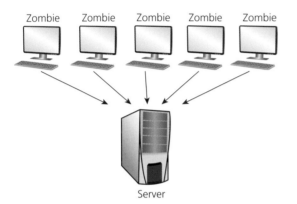

There are two main forms of denial of service a particularly nasty type of
active attack:

- attacks that consume so many network resources such as processors,
  disk space, memory, network connections, modems, that there are
  none left for legitimate users
- attacks on a specific network resource, for example attacking and
  disabling a server.

What methods are used in a denial of service attack?

Resource starvation

This means using up a network resource so that legitimate users can't
access it. A clear example is when the DOS attack sends badly assembled
packets to a network forcing the receiving network workstation or server
to hold them in its buffer, unable to process them. Eventually the buffer
area will fill up, effectively jamming the network.

Bandwidth consumption

This means flooding the network with useless traffic. An example of this
is flooding an email server with useless traffic until either it crashes or it
denies email services to legitimate users because it is so busy with the
false traffic.

Taking advantage of bugs in networking software

For example operating systems or firewalls, to crash servers.

Attacking the routers

Routers are vulnerable to PING attacks where malformed *Packet Internet Groper* packets are released onto routers. Used properly these packets are meant to help test the integrity and operating speed of a network. By releasing corrupted packets the PING attacks divert routers from their normal functions.

Domain Name Server attacks

This type of attack disrupts network access by filling the cache on Domain Name Servers with name lookup information about non-existent hosts, causing legitimate requests to be dropped. It is actually a very specific type of resource starvation.

Effects of Denial of Service (DOS) attacks

Whichever method is adopted the effects are clear: the attack disrupts use of the network and denies the legitimate users access to network services and resources. For example, email is unobtainable, data files can't be accessed, Internet access is denied.

Key points !

Security precautions

Controlling access to a computer system

The most common way of controlling access to a computer system or network is to use a system of IDs (user names) and passwords (see the screenshot on the right). You must be careful to use passwords that are hard to break. Here are the do's and don'ts of passwords.

Do	Don't
Use something you can remember.	Write it down then leave it lying about.
Use a combination of UPPER and lower case letters. You can even add numbers and punctuation, such as Isle of Skye 12?	Don't use words that are easy to guess, for example your name, your school, your football team, your favourite pop star. These sorts of passwords can be easily cracked by a hacker.
Make your password at least eight characters long.	Don't share your passwords with anyone, especially in a chat room.
Keep your username and passwords safe.	Don't email your password to anyone.
Change your password frequently.	

Password protect file(s)

Password:
••••••••••••

Confirm:
••••••••••••

OK

Cancel

Help

Warning: This password will NOT be applied to files you subsequently add to this archive.

☑ Mask Passwords(*)

Biometrics

Biometrics uses people's physical characteristics or their behaviour to identify them to a computer system. Physical characteristics are such things as fingerprints, face recognition and eye scans. Behavioural characteristics are how you walk, the sound of your voice and the way you type.

What you should know 👍

Methods for protecting your computer

Encryption

You can protect data by using encryption. This means putting the data into a code that a hacker can't understand without having the key to the code!

Encryption is especially important when transmitting sensitive data using a wireless network. This is because it is relatively easy to intercept.

Security protocols

A security protocol is a rule to control communication between networked computers. The two most commonly used are: Secure Sockets Layer (SSL) and Transport Layer Security (TLS). These both use encryption to pass data securely. They are used to provide authentication and encryption in order to send sensitive data such as credit card numbers across a network.

Security suites

Security suites are groups of programs that are designed to block the threats to your computer. A good security suite will detect and block all threats. Security suites have lots of features such as:

* anti-virus
* anti-spyware
* a firewall
* protection against worms and trojans
* identity theft protection
* spam filters.

Anti-virus software

Anti-virus software is used to prevent computer viruses from damaging computer systems. It locates the virus software and then isolates and deletes it.

Firewall

A firewall provides a means of checking all data coming into and going out of a network. The firewall decides which packets of data are allowed through to their destination address. A firewall can be:

* software running on an individual machine. You should have one on your home computer.
* software running on servers across a network (these are called **distributed firewalls**).

Firewalls are often built into your operating system or are provided by your security suite. On a large-scale network the firewall software often runs on a dedicated computer.

Questions ❓

13 What is
   a) a trojan?
   b) a virus?
   c) a worm?
14 List *two* examples of online fraud.
15 Describe *two* features of a good password.
16 Why are biometrics used to control access to computers?
17 What are security protocols used for?
18 List the features of a good security suite.

The law

The Computer Misuse Act

This Act is designed to make hacking into a computer system illegal and subject to penalties. The Act makes it an offence to *gain unauthorised access* to a computer system or to make *unauthorised modifications* to computer materials.

The Act specifies modifying computer material as:
- interfering with a system so that it doesn't run properly
- making changes to the system to prevent others accessing the system
- making changes to the software or data.

Penalties of up to five years' imprisonment and fines apply.

Copyright Designs and Patents Act 1988

This Act deals with computer software, which is now protected by law for 50 years after it is published. The Act makes it illegal to:
- make unauthorised (pirate) copies of software
- run pirate software
- transmit software over telecommunications links and copy it
- run multiple copies of software if only one copy was purchased
- give, lend or sell copies of bought software unless a licence to do so is granted.

The Data Protection Act

What you should know

The Data Protection Act

There is a need to protect people's privacy regarding information held about them on computer systems. People have the right of access to data that is held about them on computer systems. However, there are exceptions to this right to see data. For example, you have no right of access if the data is held by the Police, security forces or the Inland Revenue.

Data Protection
Act 1998

CHAPTER 29

First Published 1998
Reprinted Incorporating Corrections 2001

There are three groups of people named in the Data Protection Act. These are data subjects, data users and data controllers.

Data subjects

In the Act individuals to whom data relates are known as data subjects. Data subjects have the right to:

- know if data is held about them on a computer system and have a copy and a description of that data
- know the purposes for which the data is being processed and who is going to receive the data
- inspect such data and have it changed if they think it is inaccurate
- ask for compensation if data is inaccurate or if an unauthorised person has been given access to it
- prevent processing of data likely to cause damage or distress
- be sure that decisions made about them are not made only on the basis of automatic processing, for example psychometric testing for jobs.

For all of these the data subject can be charged a single administration fee. A data subject can apply to the courts to block the processing of data or to correct, erase or destroy it.

Data user

A data user is an individual within an organisation who makes use of personal data. The data user must keep to the following Data Protection Principles. All personal data should be:

- processed only if the consent of the individual is given, if it is part of a legal contract, if it is essential to a business transaction or the carrying out of public duties
- held for the specified purposes described in the Register entry
- accurate and where necessary kept up to date
- relevant and not excessive in relation to the purpose for which they are held
- adequate for the purpose specified
- processed in accordance with the rights of the data subject
- surrounded by proper security, like passwords and/or encryption
- transferred only to countries outside of the EU that have adequate security measures as defined in the Act.

Data controller

The data controller is defined as the person, business or organisation that controls the collection and use of personal data. The data controller must:

- register with the Data Protection Commissioner
- apply for permission to keep personal data on computers
- state what data they want to keep, its purpose and who has access to it.

Data Protection Register

Details about who holds information on members of the public on computer systems is held in the Data Protection Register which can be found in central libraries.

Data Protection Commissioner

If anyone has a problem accessing data or has a complaint about the accuracy of data, they can contact the office of the Data Protection Registrar, who oversees the administration of the Act.

Exceptions to the Act

If the data is held by the Police, the security forces or the Inland Revenue then access is denied.

The **Communications Act 2003** gives the regulation body, Ofcom, powers to legally recognise community radio stations. It also lifts restrictions on cross-media ownership and makes it illegal to use other people's wifi/broadband connections without their permission.

Questions ?

1 What is the Computer Misuse Act designed to make illegal?
2 State *two* key rights of a data subject under the Data Protection Act.
3 List *four* key principles of the Data Protection Act that a data user must stick to.
4 Who is the Data Protection Commissioner?

Health and safety

Employer regulations

The law states that an employer must:
- provide adjustable screens
- provide anti-glare screen filters
- provide adjustable chairs
- provide foot supports
- make sure lighting is suitable
- make sure workstations are not cramped
- plan work at a computer so that there are frequent breaks
- pay for appropriate eye and eyesight tests by an optician.

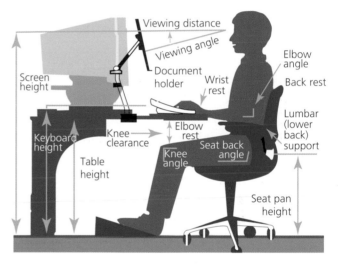

Note: These regulations do not apply to students in schools or colleges.

In order to meet these regulations, employers can use ergonomics to help them design safe and comfortable working environments for employees.

In addition, other general rules for the use of electrical appliances apply in a computer room. For example:
- There should be no trailing wires.
- Food and drink should not be placed near a machine.
- Electrical sockets must not be overloaded.
- There must be adequate space around each machine.
- Heating and ventilation must be suitable.
- Lighting must be suitable with no glare or reflections.
- Benches must be strong enough to support the computers.

What you should know 👍

How to avoid health problems

Health problem	Cause	Solution
Back problems	Sitting awkwardly at a computer	A fully adjustable chair and monitor
Repetitive Strain Injury (RSI)	Long-term use of keyboards and mouse	Take regular breaks, for example five minutes away from the computer every hour
Eye strain	Long-term staring at monitors for long periods of time	

Questions ❓

5 Describe *three* possible health problems caused by the use of computers.

6 List *three* measures that an employer must take to safeguard an employee's health.

Computers and the environment

What you should know 👍

Carbon footprint

When using a computer system you are adding to the carbon emissions being produced and released into the atmosphere. How does this happen?

★ By the amount of energy that is used to make the computer system.
★ By using electricity that is generated by using fossil fuels.

How can you help?

★ By conserving energy.
★ By buying computer systems from manufacturers who try to limit the CO_2 produced in their factories.

Energy use

Computers use lots of energy. A typical desktop PC with a 17-inch LCD monitor requires 110 watts for the computer and 35 watts for the monitor, giving a total of 145 watts.

The servers that power the Internet can use up vast amounts of energy. For example, HP's Redstone can incorporate up to 2800 servers in a rack.

This high level of energy use equals:
- high financial costs in terms of the electricity bill
- high environmental cost since it leads to extensive use of fossil fuels to produce the energy plus the consequent release of CO_2 into the atmosphere.

There are low energy alternatives, for example there are:
- PCs on the market that use as little as 25 watts of electricity

- servers that run at less than 10 watts per server
- low energy chips such as those produced by Intel.

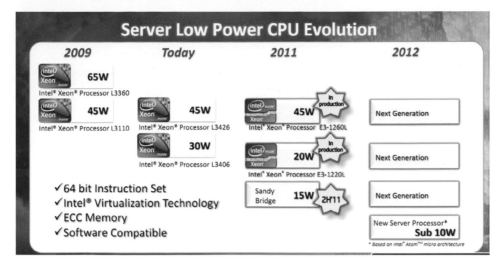

There are other ways to save energy:

- Manual power management, for example turning off computers when they are not in use.
- Using laptops where possible as they use less energy than a typical desktop: between 15 and 60 watts.

Disposal of IT equipment

It is estimated that householders and businesses in the UK dispose of more than 1 million tons of electrical and electronic equipment annually.

The disposal of IT equipment is governed by The Waste Electrical and Electronic Equipment Regulations 2006 (the WEEE Regulations). These regulations mean that:

- businesses that produce and sell electrical and electronic equipment are responsible for taking back and recovering or disposing of waste electrical and electronic equipment (WEEE) from businesses and householders
- businesses and organisations must:
  - store, collect, treat, recycle and dispose of WEEE separately from other waste
  - obtain and keep proof that the WEEE was given to an authorised waste management company, and was treated and disposed of in an environmentally sound way.

One of the problems concerning the disposal of computer systems is the need to remove personal and/or sensitive data stored on the hard drives.

This is a key security problem. Recycling centres can help with this by deleting all data stored by:

- carrying out multiple rewrites
- shredding disks.

Questions ?

7 How much energy does a typical PC use?
8 Describe *two* ways to save energy.
9 State the regulations governing the disposal of electronic equipment including computers.
10 Describe a security task that can be carried out by a recycling centre.

National 4: Added Value

Once you have finished both the Software Design and Development unit and the Information System Design and Development unit you have to complete the Added Value unit.

To do this you have to complete an assignment that will be given to you by your teacher. To complete it successfully you will have to use and develop the skills and knowledge you have acquired during both the Software Design and Development unit and the Information System Design and Development unit.

The assignment can take many forms and could include elements of, for example, programming tasks, or database development tasks, or a multimedia or web-based development task and even some research-based tasks.

To be successful you need to make sure that you have completed all of the practical tasks that your teacher has set you during the course. If you have done that then you will have developed all the practical, research and reporting skills that you will need for your assignment.

Example 🚩

Assignment: The latest smartphones

What you have to do: key points

1 Produce a plan for your assignment. This should include a design for your program and for your information system.
2 Search for and store information on four of the latest smartphones.
3 Write a program to display the above information: ask for a user's choice and the number that they want to buy, display the user's choice and the total price.
4 Either
   Create a website to display information on one of the smartphones you have researched.
   or
   Create a database to hold and process the information on each of the smartphones you have researched.
5 Keep a log or a blog of your progress through the project.
6 Test the solution and produce a report in written, electronic or oral form.

What you have to do: the details

Step 1

Choose suitable software and produce a plan with:

● timings: use suitable software to produce a list of your tasks and to indicate how long you intend to spend on each one ⇨

- an explanation of how you will get the information you need
- a list of the resources you will need to complete your tasks.

Save your plan in your portfolio folder.

Step 2

For each smartphone find key details such as:

- name
- screen size and resolution
- processor
- memory capacity
- cost.

Choose suitable software and store:

- the information you find
- the details of the sources of your information.

Save the file in your portfolio folder.

Step 3

Write a program to:

- display the information you have found on each of the four smartphones
- take in the user's choice of smartphone and the number bought
- display the user's choice and the total cost.

You should:

- Produce a design for your program.
- Implement your program.
- Test your program.
- Produce a listing of the code.
- Produce evidence of your testing and a report.

Save your design, listing and evidence of testing in your portfolio folder.

Step 4

Either

Select one of the four smartphones and produce a website advertising the smartphone and containing suitable information. (The website should have at least three linked web pages and a home page.)

You should:

- Produce a design for your website.
- Create your completed website.
- Display your website to your teacher.

Save your design document and the files for your website in your portfolio folder.

or

Design a database to hold the information and enable a user to search the database and produce simple reports.

You should:

- Produce a design for your database.
- Create your database.

⇒
- Display your database to your teacher.
- Produce evidence of simple reports from your database.

Save your design document and the files for your database in your portfolio folder.

Step 5

You should keep a log or blog of your progress by noting key details such as:

- where you got your information
- the time it took to create the program and information system
- any problems you met and how you solved them.

Evidence requirements

To complete this assignment you have to hand in the following evidence to your teacher.

1 The completed solution. This will take the form of the program listing and printouts of either your database records or your web pages and/or digital copies of your files.
2 Your log or blog. Your teacher will want to check your work by looking at your blog or log files.
3 A report on the testing of your solution in written, electronic or oral form.

National 5: Added Value

Assignment

Forty per cent of your final grade comes from a practical coursework task that you will complete in class well before you sit the exam. This task will be set by the SQA.

To complete it successfully you will have to use and develop the skills and knowledge you have acquired during both the Software Design and Development Unit and the Information System Design and Development unit.

Make sure you work at your best when completing the coursework task. It can give you a solid platform from which to tackle the exam.

External exam

Your National 5 exam is worth 60 per cent of your overall grade.

Know your topics, solve your problems

In the written exam there will be questions that check your knowledge and understanding of the topics in the course. There will also be questions on problem solving.

Exam preparation tips

- Draw up a revision plan well before the exam scheduling your revision so that you can cover it all without leaving it to the last minute.
- Use a checklist to make sure you cover all the topics.
- Learn the definitions of all the terms in this book.
- Check your knowledge is up to exam standard by answering all the questions in this book.

Appendix

Mandatory Course Content for National 5 Computing Science

The following tables list the mandatory skills, knowledge and understanding that are necessary to complete the Computing Science course at National 5. The tables are quoted from the 'National 5 Computing Science Course Assessment Specification', which is available to view online at http://www.sqa.org.uk/files_ccc/CfE_CourseAssessSpec_N5_Technologies_ComputingScience.pdf, and are reproduced by permission of SQA.

Software Design and Development	
Computational constructs	Exemplification and implementation of the following constructs: ● expressions to assign values to variables ● expressions to return values using arithmetic operations $(+, -, *, /, \wedge, \bmod)$ ● expressions to concatenate strings and arrays using the & operator ● use of selection constructs including simple and complex conditional statements and logical operators ● iteration and repetition using fixed and conditional loops ● pre-defined functions (with parameters)
Data types and structures	● String, character ● numeric (integer and real) variables ● Boolean variables ● 1-D arrays
Testing and documenting solutions	● normal, extreme and exceptional test data ● syntax, execution and logic errors ● readability of code (internal commentary, meaningful identifiers, indentation)
Algorithm specification	Exemplification and implementation of algorithms, including ● input validation
Design notations (also applies in information system design and development)	● pseudocode to exemplify programming constructs ● other contemporary design notations
Low-level operations and computer architecture	Translation of high-level program code to binary (machine code): interpreters and compilers Use of binary to represent and store: ● integers and real numbers ● characters ● instructions (machine code) ● graphics (bit-mapped and vector) Basic computer architecture: processor (registers, ALU, control unit), memory, buses (data and address), interfaces

Information System Design and Development

The following mandatory generic concepts and vocabulary may be applicable to a range of information systems types and contexts (including databases, websites, games, mobile applications, kiosk systems).

Structures and links (database)	<ul><li>database structure: flat file, linked tables, primary keys and foreign keys</li><li>field types (text, number, date, time, graphic, object, calculated, link, Boolean)</li><li>validation (including presence check, restricted choice, field length and range)</li><li>database operations search, sort (on multiple fields)</li><li>good design to avoid data duplication and modification errors (insert, delete, update)</li></ul>
Structures and links (web-based)	<ul><li>website, page, URL</li><li>hyperlinks (internal, external), relative and absolute addressing</li><li>navigation</li><li>web browsers and search engines</li><li>good design to aid navigation, usability and accessibility</li></ul>
User interface (also applies in software design and development)	User requirements (visual layout, navigation, selection, consistency, interactivity, readability)
Media types	Standard file formats:<ul><li>text: txt, rtf</li><li>audio: wav, mp3</li><li>graphics: jpeg, bmp, gif, png</li><li>video: mp4, avi</li><li>pdf</li></ul>Factors affecting file size and quality, including resolution, colour depth, sampling rate. Calculation of file size for colour bitmap. Need for compression
Coding	Exemplification and implementation of coding to create and modify information systems, including the use of:<ul><li>scripting languages (including JavaScript)</li><li>mark-up languages (including HTML)</li></ul>
Testing	<ul><li>Links and navigation</li><li>Matches user interface design</li></ul>
Purpose, features, functionality, users	<ul><li>Description of purpose</li><li>Users: expert, novice, age-range</li></ul>
Technical implementation (hardware requirements)	<ul><li>input and output devices</li><li>processor type and speed (Hz)</li><li>memory (RAM, ROM)</li><li>device type (including supercomputer, desktop, portable devices (including laptop, tablet, smartphone)</li></ul>
Technical implementation (software requirements)	<ul><li>operating systems</li><li>web browsers</li><li>specific applications and/or utilities</li></ul>
Technical implementation (storage)	<ul><li>local, web, cloud</li><li>capacity (in appropriate units)</li><li>rewritable, read-only</li><li>interface type</li><li>data transfer speed</li><li>storage devices:</li><li>built-in, external, portable</li><li>magnetic, optical</li><li>solid state</li></ul>
Technical implementation (networking/connectivity)	<ul><li>peer-to-peer, client/server</li><li>wired, optical, wireless</li></ul>
Security risks	<ul><li>spyware, phishing, keylogging</li><li>online fraud, identity theft</li><li>DOS (Denial of Service) attacks</li></ul>
Security precautions	<ul><li>anti-virus software</li><li>passwords/encryption</li><li>biometrics</li><li>security protocols and firewalls</li><li>use of security suites</li></ul>
Legal implications	Basic descriptions and implications of:<ul><li>Computer Misuse Act</li><li>Data Protection Act</li><li>Copyright, Designs and Patents Act (plagiarism)</li><li>Health and Safety regulations</li><li>Communications Act</li></ul>
Environmental impact	<ul><li>Energy use</li><li>Disposal of IT equipment</li><li>Carbon footprint</li></ul>

143

Index

Answers to Tasks and Questions

Chapter 3 Reading and Interpreting Code

1 Because it is a visual diagram the structure of the program is very clear.

2 Because it is a code-like description of the stages involved in solving the task, it helps us to write out and understand how to solve the problem.

3 a) *Dim counter As Integer:* sets up a variable called counter as an integer (whole number).

   b) The counter is used to control how many times the for . . . next loop goes round.

   c) *number_of_tickets = InputBox(" number of tickets please").* This stores data input by the user.
   price = 500. This data is *assigned,* that is it is stored by an instruction in the program.

   d) It should be indented like this:

   For counter = 1 To number_of_tickets
   names.Items.Add ("ticket number " & counter & " on " & Day & " at " & time & " price £" & price)
   Next

4 Copy and complete this table matching the type to the variable.

Variable	Type
Smartphone	String
28	Integer
130	Integer
Alexander	String
4.23	Real (single)
114.83	Real (single)

5 Boolean

6 Assign

7 A fixed loop

8 The fixed loop only repeats four times instead of six.

9 a) The error message will always be displayed even if the PIN number is correct.

   b) add an else:
   Else : MsgBox(" wrong PIN number")
   end if

   c) line 1 ' this sets up the variable PIN_ number as an integer line 3 'this uses an If to check that the number input by the user matches the value of the PIN_number assigned in line 2.

10 a) *password = InputBox(" Please enter your password")*' This inputs the user's password and stores it in the variable *password.*
   Do While password< >0 "fruitbat" ' This uses a simple condition to keep the loop running while the user's entry does not equal "fruitbat"
   password= InputBox(" Wrong password, please re-enter")
   Loop

   b) Because it would display the error message once even if the password was correct since it checks the entry at the end of the loop!

⇨

11

12

say ' you can play an animal sound or a hiphop sound'	displays the user's choice
ask ' choose a sound please' and wait	inputs the user's choice
if answer = animal	uses an *if* to check the user's choice
play sound meow	if the choice is 'animal' then a 'meow' sound is output
if answer = hiphop	uses an *if* to check the user's choice
play sound HipHop	if the choice is 'hiphop' then a 'HipHop' sound is output

13

set steps to 0	assigns value 0 to the variable steps
set pen colour to red	sets the pen colour to red
repeat until moves = 4	starts a conditional loop with a simple condition the loop will continue until the variable *moves* = 4
turn 90 degrees	turns the sprite 90 degrees
change moves by 1	adds 1 to the value of the variable moves
move 100 steps	moves 100 steps
play sound 'meow'	when the loop is finished it outputs the sound 'meow'

14 **a)** Month

    b) The while loop uses a complex condition to check the range of the month is between 1 and 12.

    c) **i)** The indentation would make it easier to read and see that if the condition failed then the user would have to input again.

        ii) It would make it easier to see that each message depended on the result of the case in the previous line.

15 **a)** To control the operation of the loop by stopping it after 24 moves or when the sprite has moved to the Y-axis position 120.

    b) Changing their values controls the position on the screen that the sprite will 'glide' to.

16

set size to answer	stores the value input by the user in the variable *size*
if size > 20	uses an *if* to check whether the value of the variable *size* is greater than 20
ask 'that's too big make it less than 21'	if it is it then outputs an error message and asks the user for another input
set size to answer	stores the value input by the user in the variable *size*
set pen size to size	assigns the value that has been checked by the *if* to the *pen size*
pen down	starts the pen writing to the screen
set pen colour to 30	assigns the value 30 to the pen colour variable
repeat 8	starts an 8 times fixed loop
move 40 steps	moves the sprite 40 steps across the screen
turn 45 degrees	turns the sprite 45 degrees

17

set eggs to 0	assigns the value 0 to the variable *eggs*
repeat until eggs>5 and eggs <13	starts a conditional with a complex condition using an '*and*' to check whether value of the eggs is between 6 and 12
ask ' enter the number of eggs you want and wait'	if the complex condition is not met then it asks the user to re-enter the number of eggs
set eggs to answer	stores the users entry in the variable *eggs*
say ' in range for 2 seconds'	outputs a message when the number of eggs entered is in the range set out in the complex condition

18 • RND gives a random real number between 0 and 1.
   • RANDOMIZE gives a new random number each time RND is used.
   • INT(grade) takes the value in the variable, here called *grade*, and drops the numbers after decimal point, i.e. INT(3.87) has the value 3.
   • ROUND(num) rounds a number to the nearest whole number.
   • LEN calculates the number of characters in a string.
   • CHR takes an ASCII value and returns the corresponding character.
   • MOD gives the remainder after an arithmetic operation.

19 In line 1, the variable number is set up to store a whole number.
   In line 2, the user enters the number to be stored in the variable price using a textbox.
   In line 3, the *If* checks to see if the number stored in the variable price is greater than 50.
   In line 4, a message is displayed if the price is greater than 50.

20 a) The variable *names* is being set up to hold text.
   b) The variable *counter* is being set up to hold whole numbers.
   c) To control how many times it goes around the loop.
   d) The user enters a name and it is stored in the variable *name*.

21 a) ' this can store numbers with decimal places, e.g. 34.56
   b) It is checking that the mark is between 0 and 100 by using a complex condition.
   c) The checked marks are being added as a running total to the variable total in line 10, then are being displayed in a textbox in line 11.

22 a) String variables to hold text
   b) To hold the initial letters of the names being entered in lines 3 and 4
   c) The first letter of the *firstname*
   d) The initial letters of the names being entered in lines 3 and 4

23 **a)** An array with five spaces to hold text

   b) An array with five spaces to hold whole numbers

   c) i) To control how many times the *For ... next* loop runs

   ii) To step down the *name* array

   d) It uses the index to step down the array and adds the names in the array to a listbox.

24 **a)** It is checking whether the contents of the variable *waistsize* are greater than 60.

   b) The complex condition checks whether the contents of the variable *waistsize* are between 31 and 39.

   c) It outputs the text 'Medium' to the screen using a textbox.

Answers

Chapter 6 Creating an Information System

1 Records and fields

2 ● Numeric fields to hold numbers, for example exam marks.

   ● Text fields to hold words, for example forenames of pupils.

   ● Graphic fields to hold images, for example photographs.

   ● Date fields to hold dates, for example date of birth.

   ● Time fields to hold times, for example start time of exam.

   ● Calculated fields: to hold a formula to calculate averages or totals, for example.

3 **a)** You would include a Boolean field if you wanted to test whether a condition was true or false.

   b) A link field is used for storing links to files on:

   ● your computer

   ● a network

   ● the Internet.

4 To uniquely identify a record

5 **a)** A URL is the unique address of a web page.

   b) A hyperlink is the means of linking to other web pages.

6 An external hyperlink links you to a web page on another website.

7 A well-designed navigation system will:

   ● have a range of text and graphic-based hyperlinks sprinkled throughout the website to make moving about as flexible as possible

   ● have a navigation bar with clear links to different areas of the website

   ● have a site map, for visitors to the website who may need a little more navigational help, that lists all the sections and web pages, as well as a shorter path to the different areas for those who know what exactly they are looking for

   ● be consistent throughout the website. This will help users to learn, through repetition, how to get around the website.

8 The purpose of a browser is to help you navigate the World Wide Web, to move between and view web pages.

9 **a)** It is needed to enable the processor to communicate with the external devices.

   b) Any two of: changes electrical voltages, deals with control signals, changes analogue data to digital form, stores incoming data so that the processor can get on with other tasks.

10 The more information you have about your target audience the better you will be able to design an interface that they will find easy to use.

⇨

11 a) Young children: The most commonly used functions and outputs should be readily accessible with plenty of feedback, online help and tutorials easily available. This could be done, for example, by using simple toolbars with rows of clear icons, a navigation bar or an easy-to-use search box and a touch screen.

b) Experienced users: One approach is to present the most common options in a menu but allow an experienced user to personalise by selecting/adding other options and features. In terms of input an experienced user would be more likely to interact with the system using a keyboard and mouse to enter commands or keyboard shortcuts.

c) An elderly person may well have trouble with their eyesight and so colour balance, text size and style as well as simple instructions and a touch screen will be required.

12 Make an interface more interactive by using a selection of:
- feedback to step users through a process or alert them to errors
- hotspots to trigger actions
- links clear with meaningful link text
- interactive animations
- video clips
- sound files
- polls or quizzes.

13 You would use the same:
- terms throughout
- sounds to alert an input error, for example
- mouse action or command to produce the same action
- font and font size
- graphics style and size
- navigation bar in the same location on each web page
- text alignment.

Answers

Chapter 7 Scripting and Mark-up Languages

1 A mark-up language is a language used to create web pages.
2 Any suitable HTML
3 Scripts are small programs that can automate tasks by creating a macro or generate dynamic content for web pages.
4 VBscript, Applescript, PHP
5 JavaScript is used to add interactivity to HTML pages and to create 'cookies'.
6 Any suitable script

Answers

Chapter 8 Adding Text, Graphics, Sound and Video

1. **a)** $(4 \times 4 \times 300 \times 300 \times 8)$ bits = 11520000 bits = 1440000 bytes = 1406 Kbytes = 1.373 Mbytes
   b) 4.119 Mbytes
2. GIF is limited to 256 colours.
3. Lossless compression
4. Lossy compression: parts of the image are cut out in such a way that they will not be noticed by the human eye.
5. Unless they are compressed sound files can be very large, particularly if they have a high sampling frequency and bit depth.
6. Sampling frequency is how often the sound is sampled in a second. Sampling depth is the number of bits, or bytes, used to store a single sample.
7. A WAV file can be sampled at a bit depth of either 8 bits or 16 bits with a frequency of 11.025 KHz, 22.05 KHz, or 44.1 KHz. This means files can be very large since they are not compressed. MP3 files are compressed using a lossy compression technique, commonly compressing to around 1/20 the size of the equivalent WAV file.
8. An uncompressed 30-second video clip, taken at 25 frames per second (fps), with a resolution of 640×480 and shot in 24-bit colour will be 659.2 Mb in size.
9. AVI has no built in compression and has a file size limit of 2 Gb. MPEG uses lossy compression and can compress a two-hour video into a few Gigabytes.
10. It demands less storage space and will be quicker to transmit across a network.
11. It is a standard file format that includes all the information about styles, fonts, sizes, paragraphing and indentation.
12. It is widely used for sharing and publishing documents across the Internet.

Answers

Chapter 9 Hardware

1. The processor is the 'brain' of the computer that deals with all the movement of data and any calculations to be carried out.
2. RAM loses its data and ROM does not.
3. MHz and GHz
4. 640MHz
5. 120 * 1024 = 122880
6. RAM memory loses its contents when the system is powered down. Backing storage retains its contents and often has greater capacity.
7. CD-ROM stores 700 Mb and a single-layer, single-sided DVD-ROM 4.7Gb.
8. Storing data that you want to be easily portable between systems
9. To backup data on the main hard drive and to extend storage capacity
10. **a)** joystick
    b) mouse
    c) webcam
    d) microphone
11. Any suitable printer
12. Any suitable screen

$\Rightarrow$

13 A laptop is light, portable and can be powered by batteries. A desktop cannot be moved and is powered using your mains electricity supply.

14 Supercomputers have thousands of processors and very large memory capacity which is measured in terabytes.

15 Any three of: a mobile phone with, for example a memory to hold an address book and ring tones; the ability to send and receive and store text messages; a multimedia device that can handle text, graphics and audio and video, has a browser to access web pages and send email, has a digital camera to capture images and send them through the phone network and even the Internet, can play MP3 files and games; can connect with laptops and desktops.

16 A flat touch screen usually between 7 and 10 inches in size, a screen resolution commonly around 1200 × 800, a processor with a speed around 1.5 GHz.

17 Any four of: manages the use of both the internal memory and the backing storage; manages the files and keeps track of where they are stored in the system; provides the user with an interface, usually a graphics-based interface; increasingly with a touch screen and even voice input; runs other software; controls the use of devices such as printers.

18 Any accurate description of home or school system

Answers

Chapter 10 Networks and Security

1 Local Area Network

2 School, office, library, hospital, factory, etc. Any location in one building or limited area.

3 Fibre-optic cable transmits at *very* high speeds. It also doesn't lose data because of interference and is very secure. It is very expensive to install.

4 They are easy to install, as there is no need for cables. Also, you can move around when you work without trailing wires.

5 The Internet is a global system of interconnected computer networks.

6 Any three: World Wide Web, search engines, forums, chat rooms, social networking.

7 a) On their own hard drives, optical storage, servers that they have to maintain and update
   b) Users rent storage space on servers.

8 A business does not need to spend large amounts of money buying and installing expensive computer systems and networks in order to access powerful computing resources.

9 They worry that data stored in the 'Cloud' will be hacked into.

10 a) Each workstation stores its data on a local hard drive or optical storage drive.
   b) Data is stored centrally on a server.

11 a) A workstation operated by a user
   b) A computer that controls a resource and makes it available to clients on the network

12 It will be managed centrally by a server that will be tasked with holding all the security data and software.

13 a) Trojan: A program that looks harmless and tricks the user into running it on their computer. It then carries out its real task, such as displaying adverts on the desktop or installing unwanted toolbars.
   b) Virus: A computer virus is a program that makes copies of itself, attaches itself to programs the user has installed on their computer, and then damages the system.
   c) Worm: Similar to a virus, a worm is a program that makes copies of itself and then spreads through a network in order to damage systems as it goes along.

⇨
14 Any two, for example: bank card and cheque fraud, charity donation fraud, identity fraud, inheritance fraud, loan scams, Lottery scams, online shopping fraud, work from home scams.
15 At least eight letters long, has upper and lower cases, numbers and even punctuation.
16 They are unique identifiers.
17 They are rules to control communication between networked computers.
18 A good security suite should have anti-virus, anti-spyware, a firewall, protection against worms and trojans, identity theft protection, spam filters.

Answers

Chapter 11 The Law and the Environment

1 This Act is designed to make hacking into a computer system illegal and subject to penalties.
2 Any two from: to know if data is held about them on a computer system; to have a copy and a description of that data; to inspect such data; to have it changed if they think it is inaccurate.
3 Data must be:
   ● processed only if the consent of the individual is given
   ● accurate and where necessary kept up to date
   ● relevant and not excessive in relation to the purpose for which it is held
   ● surrounded by proper security, like passwords and/or encryption.
4 The Data Protection Commissioner oversees the administration of the Act.
5 Back problems, Repetitive Strain Injury, eye strain
6 Provide adjustable screens, anti-glare screen filters, adjustable chairs, foot supports
7 145 watts
8 Use low power PCs or laptops; switch off computers when not in use
9 Businesses that produce and sell electrical and electronic equipment are responsible for taking back and recovering or disposing of waste electrical and electronic equipment (WEEE) from businesses and householders. Businesses and organisations must:
   ● store, collect, treat, recycle and dispose of WEEE separately from other waste
   ● obtain and keep proof that the WEEE was given to an authorised waste management company, and was treated and disposed of in an environmentally sound way.
10 Deleting sensitive data by carrying out multiple rewrites and shredding disks.